The Complete Guide to

CROSS-COUNTRY
SKIING

in Canada

The Complete Guide to CROSS-COUNTRY SKIING in Canada

John Peaker

1986

Doubleday Canada Limited, Toronto, Ontario

Doubleday & Company, Inc., Garden City, New York

Illustrations by Bo Kim Louie
Cover photo © John P. Kelly/The Image Bank Canada
Jacket design by Dragon's Eye Press
Typesetting by Alpha Graphics Limited
Printed and bound in Canada by Gagne Printing Limited

Canadian Cataloguing in Publication Data
Peaker, John
The complete guide to cross-country skiing in Canada

ISBN 0-385-25101-7

1. Cross-country skiing—Canada. I. Title.

GV854.8.C3P43 1986   796.93'0971   C86-094046-2

Library of Congress Cataloging-in-Publication Data

Peaker, John.
  The complete guide to cross-country skiing in Canada.

  Includes index.
    1. Cross-country skiing—Canada—Guide-books.
2. Canada—Description and travel—1981–   —Guide-
books. I. Title.
GV854.8.C2P43 1986   796.93'0971   86-16654
ISBN 0-385-25101-7

To my family:
Sandra, Kelli, and Kevin

Contents

Preface   9

PART ONE: GETTING STARTED   13
 1. **Equipment**   15
    Skis   15
    Boots and Bindings   20
    Poles   29
    Clothing and Other Necessities   31
 2. **Waxing**   35
    Simple Waxing   36
    The Variables   38
    The Waxing Process   39
    Progressive Waxing Techniques   41
 3. **Training**   43
    Firming Up   43
    Cardiovascular Fitness   44
    Roller Skiing, Roller Skating, and Training Gadgets   47
    Your First Times Out on the Trail   49

PART TWO: MASTERING SKI SKILLS   53
 4. **How to Develop Your Technique**   55
    Skiing Downhill   55
    Diagonal Stride   56
    Variations on the Diagonal Stride   57
    Skating Technique   58
    Slowing Down and Stopping   59
    Falling and Getting Up After a Fall   60
    Turning   61
    Climbing Techniques   67
 5. **Telemarking**   70
    How to Do the Telemark Turn   71
    Telemarking Equipment   73
 6. **Non-Competitive Touring**   75
    Touring Tips   75
    Family Touring   77
 7. **Seniors: The New Breed of Cross-Country Skiers**   82

PART THREE: THE COMPETITIVE EDGE   85
 8. **Competitive Touring and Citizens' Races**   87
    Preparation and Planning for Marathons   87
    The Marathon Race: Strategies   90
    Events in Canada   91
    Incentive Award Programs in Canada   95
 9. **Marathon Skiing: A Personal Glimpse**   98
10. **Racing**   105
    Shaping Up in the Off-Season   105
    On-Snow Training   112
    Racing Techniques   114
    Racing Advice   121
11. **Happiness is Spring Skiing**   126

PART FOUR: PRACTISING YOUR SKIING SKILLS   129
12. **Where to Ski in Canada**   131
    Newfoundland and Labrador   131
    Prince Edward Island   133
    Nova Scotia   134
    New Brunswick   134
    Quebec   141
    Ontario   145
    Manitoba   199
    Saskatchewan   199
    Alberta   201
    British Columbia   223
    Northwest Territories   227
    Yukon   227

Appendices   229
 1. The Latest in Touring and Light Touring Skis   231
 2. Racing Skis   235
Special Acknowledgment   243
Index   245

Preface

I HAVE WRITTEN *The Complete Guide to Cross-Country Skiing in Canada* for those who want to experience the exhilaration of gliding effortlessly along a winding trail on a frosty, picturesque winter morning and who want to derive the full benefits and joys from this unique sport. The experience of being in complete harmony with nature will rejuvenate you physically and mentally, and you'll feel like a "free spirit."

Anyone, regardless of age, can enjoy the magnificent sport of cross-country skiing. If you have been reluctant until now about venturing out into "the great white north" or have not known where to go in Canada to find the ski trails most suited to your needs, this book is for you. I hope that it will help you join the ever-increasing number of Canadians who are taking up the sport of cross-country skiing. According to Statistics Canada, there are now a greater number of cross-country skiing enthusiasts than there are downhill skiers!

The Complete Guide to Cross-Country Skiing in Canada is also aimed at those hardy souls who have done some recreational skiing and who would like to learn more about the touring and racing aspects of the sport, and the satisfying rewards these bring.

Cross-country skiing can be enjoyed and savored by every member of the family. Probably the most appealing aspect of the sport is that it can become a lifetime pursuit. At this printing, the legendary Herman "Jackrabbit" Smith-Johannsen, the "patriarch" of cross-country skiing in North America, is still skiing at the age of 111 years.

My book and my passionate love for the sport of cross-country skiing are a direct result of my admiration for and the inspiration provided by "Jackrabbit," the "pied piper of the ski trails." During a recent conversation with him, I asked if he had skied this year. He replied tersely, but enthusiastically, "Of course! Skied in April at the cabin. Conditions were wonderful!"

Herman Smith-Johannssen was born in Norway on June 15, 1875. He started to ski at two years of age. In his youth he participated in cross-country, jumping, and slalom events just outside of Oslo. As a graduate engineer, Herman accepted a posting in the United States with an American firm and was soon transferred to northern Canada to be a special machinery representative during the building of the Grand Trunk Railway.

Jackrabbit's travels took him into the remote wilderness north of Lake Superior and into Quebec, where the only methods of travel were sled and snowshoes. His discovery that the area was inhabited mainly by the Cree forced him to use all his resourcefulness. He soon learned the Cree language and befriended the native people. At first the Cree laughed at Herman's skinny skis and funny-looking "sticks" (poles). It didn't take long, however, for Herman to prove that his skis were faster than their snowshoes. Twenty years later when he returned, the Cree were using skis and the snowshoes were strapped to their backs.

Years later, after sojourns in Cuba and New York, Herman settled with his wife Alice and his three children in Lake Placid, New York, an area that reminded him of his native Norway. It was at Lake Placid that cross-country skiing originated in the eastern United States. Herman made a great contribution to the rise in popularity of the sport by carving out numerous ski trails and by promoting mass participation in cross-country skiing, jumping, and downhill skiing.

While living at Lake Placid, Herman frequently commuted to Montreal on business and fell in love with the Laurentians. In 1928, he relocated his entire family in Montreal. The following year disaster struck Herman as it did so many others; the stock market crash wiped him out financially. Emotionally spent, he retreated with his family to a small cabin in Shawbridge, approximately three miles from his present cabin in Piedmont.

At Shawbridge in the early years of the Depression, Jackrabbit developed the famous Maple Leaf Trail, which extends some eighty miles from Labelle in Shawbridge. The trail was laid from one hotel to the next: a network of trails many years ahead of its time. He also participated in the first ascent of Mont Tremblant by other than native peoples in April, 1930, and was instrumental in the cutting of many downhill runs including the Tashereau and Kandahar downhills on Mont Tremblant.

Jackrabbit honed his hunting skills and always had moose or deer hanging in the shed. He had no car, no phone, and no refrigerator. It was "survival of the fittest." Strangely enough, it was during this time of extreme hardship that Jackrabbit discovered true happiness. The hard times brought the family closer together than ever before. During the winter, Jackrabbit's cross-country skis carried him over the frozen terrain. In summer, he traveled by canoe to hunt and fish in his wild paradise.

Jackrabbit soon found that his knowledge of skiing was keenly sought after by people from all walks of life. He felt useful and satisfied in helping people to learn about nature and was proud of the fact that he could impart his knowledge of cross-country skiing to others.

Jackrabbit's level of physical fitness and stamina exemplify what a healthy, active life can bring in terms of vigor and well-being. His feats in the cross-country skiing world are legendary. When he was fifty years old, competing against top college athletes, he placed second in the only sanctioned twenty-five-mile ski race in the United States. At sixty years of age, while helping to coach the Canadian Olympic team, he amazed the athletes during a training run by keeping up with the best cross-country skiers Canada could produce at that time. In his seventies, he continued to compete in cross-country races, leaving skiers less than one-third his age looking at the tails of his skis. At age eighty-five, Jackrabbit led a group of skiers on a two-hour trek, and returned them exhausted to his cabin for lunch and rest. An hour later he was back on the trail with another group of skiers, extolling the virtues of the sport and helping them to understand the phenomena of the wilderness.

Jackrabbit "the Magnificent" has had dozens of honors showered on him over the years, including a Doctor of Law degree, Member of the Order of Canada, induction into the Canadian

Sports Hall of Fame, and the Dubonnet Skier of the Year award. Personally I suspect that he is most honored by the title *"Oka-makum Wapooes"* bestowed on him by the Cree. It means simply "Chief Jackrabbit."

Jackrabbit's contribution to the sport of cross-country skiing can be summed up in one word: awesome. I sincerely hope that my own contribution, *The Complete Guide to Cross-Country Skiing in Canada*, will serve as an honest extension of the leadership shown by Jackrabbit Smith-Johannsen.

Part One
Getting Started

Equipment and Clothing •
Waxing • Training •
The First Time Out

The sport of cross-country skiing is an art in itself, and even after thirty years' experience one still learns something new every time out. Cross-country skiing introduces one to hundreds of people from all walks of life. This old "jackrabbit" still corresponds with many acquaintances from past tours and races. Cross-country skiers are a friendly and close-knit group of individuals. There is always a special experience that every skier wants to share with another. Even discussing the wax of the day opens the door to new friendships.

Cross-country skiing is rated as one of the best all-round conditioners for the human body. Because of the high repetition rate of the arms and legs, both are strengthened as you tack on those kilometers week after week. Depending on your weight and pace, you will burn off fifteen to twenty calories every minute you are in motion on the trails. The body takes on a "sculptured" look as stomach muscles tighten up. As your cardiovascular capacity improves, so does your stamina.

Skiing demands strength, stamina, agility, and cardiovascular fitness. These four attributes must be patiently and gradually developed. I know that it won't be long before you, too, will be extolling the virtues of this unique sport to others. These next chapters on equipment and training will help you get started.

Chapter One
Equipment

YOU'VE HEARD OF "STAR WARS," now come "Ski Wars." As I write this book, high technology is progressing at a faster rate than anyone could have imagined. Almost daily there are new break-throughs in skis, boots, binding systems, and poles. Every man-ufacturer is after a "first" in its specialty. The cross-country boom even has downhill-ski manufacturers after the lucrative cross-country ski market. Cross-country skiers are no longer being treated as second-class citizens who ski on barrel staves. Cross-country enthusiasts welcome this trend with open arms because it means improved ski equipment and, ultimately, better skiing for everyone.

Skis

To Wax or Not to Wax?
Many people ask me: "Should I buy no-wax skis or regular skis that require waxing?" My answer is, it depends. For children aged six to ten, waxless skis or those with "fish scales" are ideal to start with. They require no waxing, which saves adults the time-consuming task of wax application. The youngsters can put on the skis any time and not have the problem of slipping back on the snow. Young skiers rarely have the patience or time to

worry about such details as waxing. They want to ski instantly without any hassles. Waxless skis give them this benefit.

For older children, teenagers, and most adults, I do not recommend waxless skis for the following reasons. Waxless skis inhibit the ability to glide, both on the flat and downhill. On hard-packed and icy surfaces, they do not provide the necessary grip for a proper "kick." If you plan on entering tours and are intent on improving your technique, I recommend regular touring skis that require waxing.

Fit

In the past, the only rule of thumb used in fitting skis was that the tips should come up to your wrist when your arm is extended over your head. The wrist measurement method is only a starting point. In reality fitting skis has more to do with weight than arm reach. It's better to have a ski with the right camber than to worry about the length. The camber refers to the arc in the skis just under the foot area. Too much camber in relation to your weight would make it difficult to "weigh down," or flatten the ski against the snow. Consequently it would be difficult to attain a proper "kick," and you would constantly be sliding backwards. Too little camber would mean that a poor glide is likely because the "kicking" area would be flat against the snow, even on downhills.

In order to find the proper camber, place the skis that you want to test on the floor. Place a piece of paper under the foot area. Stand on both skis with equal weight distribution. Have someone move the paper back and forth. If it moves freely that means that the midsections of the skis will not ride on the snow and hold you back. Now put all your weight on one ski and try to remove the paper. If the paper slips out easily you have too much camber or the camber is too "stiff." Find a pair with "softer" camber, which won't let the paper budge when all your weight is on one ski.

As far as the length of your skis is concerned, the table on the following page should serve as a general guide.

Be cautious about the type of skis you buy. Metal-edged skis are used for downhill skiing at ski lift areas and for icy back-country skiing. Wide side-cut skis are too wide for use on machine-groomed tracks.

Your height	Ski length
5'–5'6"	185 cm
5'7"–5'9"	190 cm
5'10"–5'11"	195 cm
6'	205 cm
6'1"–6'4"	210 cm
over 6'4"	215 cm

Construction

The first skis were made of a simple piece of handcrafted wood. Then came skis constructed of *laminated wood*, which was easier to manufacture. It allowed the flexibility of using a variety of woods. The core was usually a light wood and all surfaces hardwood, producing a lighter, more durable ski.

In the *fiberglass-reinforced* ski, fiberglass-reinforced plastic replaces wood as the load-carrying element. This ski is available in two different types of core construction: a wood bi-flow core with an air-channel system to make it lighter, or a combined wood/foam construction called box construction. This ski has quite a few glued joints.

The foam core fiberglass ski has become popular among racers and good recreational skiers because of its lightness and good gliding characteristics. This construction method, which uses synthetic expanded material, is advantageous because it does not have any wood, which can be moisture sensitive. The ski's ability to reject moisture is important, as the amount of moisture absorbed is directly related to the speed of the ski. It stands to reason that the less moisture is absorbed, the less energy will be required to push the ski forward during the kick-and-glide process. Maximum forward thrust can thus be better maintained.

The foam core fiberglass ski is vulnerable to fatigue cracks, however, and is more difficult to "hold" when in the kick position. A full plastic core construction ski that contains materials that already hold some moisture has a lower reaction speed and holds better in the kick position. A good recreational or beginner ski should be flexible with a soft camber.

Skis may have a *sidecut*, or be *parallel cut* or *negative sidecut*. *Sidecut* means that the ski is broader across its tip and tail than at its middle. This makes an arc that supposedly helps you turn. All Alpine ski manufacturers use a sidecut. Sidecut skis are used in Telemark skiing or off-trail skiing. *Parallel cut* skis are the same width tip to tail and are ideal for in-track skiing, because there is less friction at the tip and tail areas with the sides of the ski tracks than with a sidecut ski. *Negative sidecut* is found only on racing skis. Negative sidecut means that the tips and tails are much narrower than the middle. The narrow tips offer less wind resistance and therefore make the skis much faster. Negative sidecut skis are used only in machine-groomed preset tracks.

Camber refers to the upward bow of the ski along its base. It allows the midportion of the ski to ride up off the snow when the ski is gliding. When pushed down during the kick, the ski's camber should flatten out for a moment under the skier's full weight. This allows the wax or waxless pattern (in the case of waxless skis) to grip for the forward kick.

Forebody flex refers to how firm or flexible the ski is when you hold its midsection and pull back strongly on the forward end. A fairly stiff forebody flex helps you turn and holds the ski firmly throughout a turn.

Tip and tail flex is self-explanatory. When shopping for touring skis, it is wise to consider a pair of skis that have relatively stiff tail sections. Such skis ensure that your weight is supported when you sit back on your skis to go downhill or around tight, fast corners.

P-Tex refers to the brand name of the base produced by the best-known manufacturer of ski bases. There are many other base manufacturers who use similar versions of the polyethylene material. The quality of P-Tex is indicated by the higher number; for example, P-Tex 2000 is more durable and has better wax retention than P-Tex 1000.

When someone asks whether a base is *patterned* or *smooth*, they are referring to the base on waxless skis. The patterned base class really has two base classifications: positive and negative. A positive base is raised above the level of the rest of the base. Positive bases are considered fairly efficient for gripping corn snow (small icy pellets) and old snow and can be used in temperatures around the freezing mark. An example of a positive base is Trak's Omnitrack. A negative pattern base is one in which the base is cut down into the skis' base material. This base is considered good for colder and softer snow. Fischer's Crown base is a popular negative base.

A smooth base on waxless skis is one that has been chemically or electronically treated. The temperature and snow crystals react on the base in such a manner that it raises small hairs to grip the snow. (These hairs, incidentally, do not interfere with the glide.) Some of the brand name smooth bases include Multigrade, Neverwax, and Laser.

Racing Skis

If you are racing every week and are committed to a top performance every time out, the expense of a high-performance model may be justified for you. If you're not racing on a regular basis but would rather concentrate on a few long or medium distance events over the course of the season, a light, competitive touring ski will probably suffice and will be easier on the pocketbook as well. As you review the performance summaries of the different models in Appendix One at the end of this book, think of your own strengths and weaknesses and be honest with yourself. In so doing, you will be better able to match yourself up with a pair of skis that will ultimately lead to improved performances.

When purchasing racing skis you must consider your weight, your technical ability, and your past experience. When a 170-pound skier of average ability kicks off on one ski, he exerts one and one-half times his body weight, or 255 pounds of pressure, on the kicking ski. When gliding, he has one-half of his body weight, or 85 pounds, on each ski. The 85-pound weight balance represents the softest cambered racing skis' *first-touch* value.

First touch is the number of pounds of direct pressure on the balance point required to make a ski's wax pocket "first touch" the snow. In other words, it means that anyone up to 170 pounds could use that ski and be reasonably sure that there would be no wax-pocket drag during the glide phase because the kick area of the ski would ride above the surface of the snow. Consequently you'll want a ski with a first-touch reading of at least one-half of your body weight; any lower reading will cause the wax pocket to drag on the snow when gliding on both skis.

Racers and serious tourers who are considering the purchase of racing skis have presumably refined their technique to a point at which any racing skis would work adequately for them. It should be noted, however, that there is a wide variation in performance values. The stiffest cambered ski tested was nearly twice as stiff as the softest. If you weigh approximately 170 pounds, have been race/touring for four to five years, and have trained with weights, you will probably find one of the stiffer models more rewarding.

Boots and Bindings

Take your time buying boots. Try on several makes and find a pair that feels snug and comfortable. Try on the boots while wearing a single pair of socks so you will be able to get a better feel inside the boot. There should be about a quarter of an inch of toe space at the front of the boot. Walk around on them. Stop and pretend you are skiing in them. Do the heels slip?

Make sure you know what you are buying. For cross-country skiing you want a light touring boot, not heavy, rigid Telemarking boots. Boots come in high-cut (eight inches or more), mid-cut (six inches), and low-cut (three or four inches) heights. High-cut boots are designed for off-track, deep snow, or Telemark skiing. They are usually made with top-grain leather uppers with a polyester or soft leather lining. Many of the high-cut boots have full-length steel or plastic shanks for torsional stability. Mid-cut boots are a reduced version of the high-cut with less torsional rigidity. They are also more flexible for forward motion. Low-cut boots or touring boots have torsionally rigid plastic or polycarbonate soles. The uppers are either all-leather or a combination of leather and nylon.

During the 1970s most boots would fit most bindings because boots and bindings were "compatible" within three classifications: 75/12 Nordic Norm, 50/12 Touring Norm, and 50/7 Racing Norm. The first number refers to the width of the boot's toe piece and binding housing opening, the second number refers to the thickness of the boot's sole. Compatible meant that you could buy almost any manufacturer's boot and fit it to any manufacturer's binding. Life was simple way back in the 1970s.

Even during this period, however, the high-performance racers and innovators felt that there was a better way than the Nordic norm boot/binding system. Racers wanted boots that were lighter but had the same torsional stability. They also wanted a lighter, more streamlined binding that was durable. With the advent of new boot/binding systems for racers trying to shave seconds off their best times, the Nordic Norm was being seriously challenged. When these innovative new systems proved to be both popular and successful with the racers, a number of companies began to market them to the recreational skier.

In the early 1980s, consumer interest in the "incompatibles"— boot and binding systems that mated only to each other—really took off. Interest in the Nordic Norm declined as the recreational skier came to prefer the feel, the appearance, and the new sleek performance of these new systems. The former standard toe piece width of 50 mm was reduced to a width of 38 mm. "Norm" was never to be normal again. Now you can see why it isn't that simple to recommend individual brands of boots!

Today technology dictates that we discuss systems: boot/binding systems. After years of battling for control of the incompatible system, a French company emerged above the rest. In 1981, the French alpine boot and binding specialist, Salomon, hit the market with a revolutionary new system called the Salomon Nordic System (SNS). The target market was racers.

Salomon, who had been working on this system for almost a decade, circumvented the elongated toe piece and introduced a snub-nosed toe inset with a square wire bail. The wire bail fitted over a metal binding post and was held in place by a plastic closure tab. For increased control, a single slot under the ball of the foot meshed with a single top wedge-plate. The keel was flat— no wedge and groove.

The feature that really created a sensation among racers, however, was the plastic binding flex-plate located directly under the toe piece receptacle on the binding. On each forward lift, the flex-plate moved with the skier's foot movement. The new flexibility added immensely to the power of the forward thrust. The SR90 boot and binding were a great success story. One year later, Salomon added a touring binding with a stiffer flex-plate that afforded more control as well as a touring boot with the SNS boot/binding combination.

Now, the companies that laughed at the Salomon system are desperately trying to catch up to the leader. A few of the new brand names to remember include Contact, Control, ALS, and System F.

Contact

The Contact system by Trak uses a main housing that is hinged. Each time the skier kicks, the entire unit pivots upward. As a result the binding's sidewalls are always in contact with the boot, thereby affording extra stability. The kicking action takes place against a rubber flexor set in between the binding's base plate and main housing. An added feature is that two sets of removable flexors of different hardness come with each Contact binding. These flexors allow you to set exactly the amount of pressure you want to push against when kicking.

Contact boots have plastic soles that are grooved lengthwise under the ball of the foot and heel. The grooves fit tightly over the ridges of a ski-mounted plate for improved control on the corners and during herringbones and skating. With the Contact racing boot, the grooved heel fits over a wedge-shaped mounted heel on the top of the ski. This feature allows for even better control. Contact touring and light touring bindings offer a choice of either the wedged heel piece or a spiked, mounted plate that grips the boot heel.

Like the Salomon system, the toe pieces on Contact boots are stubby. Two side slots fit over plastic bars in the binding housing. To secure the binding to your boot, all you have to do is step down. The bindings are released by simply pushing the tip of one of your poles against the front part of the flexor.

At last count there were three Contact bindings from which to choose. They are the 401 ultralight for racers, the 301 light touring binding, and the 202 binding for average touring.

In addition to the variety of bindings, Trak also offers several different boots. The CS400 is a super-light nylon and leather racing boot. The CS250 is all-leather with a Gore-Tex and Thinsulate lining and is designed for light touring. A regular touring boot, the CS100 is an all-purpose touring boot with polyurethane-coated leather.

Control

Manufactured by Alpina, the Control system uses a new boot sole along with a unique new binding. The boot soles feature slots across the sole to increase flexibility. The front of the sole tip is raised and has a groove across the bottom that enables it to fit over a ridge in the Control binding.

The Control binding itself has a sizable square ridge under the ball of the foot with a latch-type binding at the toe. The heel piece is separate and square in shape. The fit between boot and binding is enhanced by the fact that the boot's sole also has square grooves under the ball of the foot and at the heel. These grooves fit over the ski-top mounted plates, thereby giving added ski control.

Alpina currently offers six models of Control boots from which to choose. Naturally they all fit into the Control System binding. There are two series of boots—the CSL boots and the CSN—each of which offers a low-cut racing boot, a mid-cut light touring boot, and a high-cut general touring boot. The three CSL boots are fleece- and Thinsulate-lined while the CSN boots are Velutina- and Thinsulate-lined.

ALS

ALS is a result of the amalgamated efforts of an Italian boot manufacturer named Artex and a Norwegian ski manufacturer named Landsem. The ALS system is marketed under the name "System F." The ALS system, like the Salomon Nordic System, employs a metal piece in the toe rather than a shaped plastic toe piece like Contact and Control.

ALS boots have plastic soles. Short pins protrude from each side of the stunted toe piece. The pins fit into grooves in the aluminum binding housing. Here's how it works: as you push down into the binding with the boot toe piece, the spring-loaded binding housing opens to accept the boot's toe piece and then closes over it.

The ALS system, like the others, has a double-ridged plate on top of the ski that fits into matching grooves on the soles for added turning control. There is neither a flex-plate nor a flexor.

ALS boots from Nor Tur include a high-cut, all-leather, Gore-Tex-lined touring boot and three racing boots. You can select either a leather, a Gore-Tex/leather or a fabric/leather racing boot.

Salomon

The SNS (Salomon Nordic System) has not seen any dramatic changes at this writing, but with this company's past reputation for innovation, look for new breakthroughs in the near future.

There are, however, new Salomon boot models to choose from this year. Before we take a look at what's available, I should point out that Salomon has appointed SNS licensees to market their products. The licensees include the following companies: Merrell, Heirling, Norboot, Alfa, Jolas, and Majola.

Salomon's latest boot models include the SR901 and ultralight SR901 Equipe racing boots. The 901 boots have light leather uppers backed with insulating polyurethane foam and brushed polyester fabric. Boot stability and protection have been improved by reinforcing the toe boxes with canvas. The 901 Equipe is, to date, the lightest cross-country boot on the market. At approximately 250 grams per pair, it is made from ultralight polyester mesh. This boot is used exclusively for racing. Both the 901 and the 901 Equipe have the standard Salomon laced inner boot which is covered by an outer boot layer and cinched down with Velcro.

Merrell SNS boots are designed mainly for general touring and offer some definite advantages, particularly the SNS compatible high-cut touring boot called Velcro SNS. This boot features a system of three straps with Velcro closures that enable you to loosen the boots easily and quickly when you stop for a break.

The other additions to the Merrell line, the Velcro SNS and the Sight Touring SNS with the traditional lace-and-hook system, have soft one-piece leather uppers and glove leather liners.

Heirling's SNS newcomers include a mid-cut, top-grain leather boot called Davos and an all-leather high-cut boot for off-track skiing called Nordic Trail.

For women, who generally have a narrower last, Norboot has developed the Lady Norski high-cut. This boot is all leather with a Velcro closure leather strap across the top of the ankle for added support. There is good news generally for all tourers with narrower feet. The new Alfa 1316, a mid-cut, all-leather SNS boot, is made to fit skinny feet and is even fleece-lined.

Another Salomon SNS licensee, Jolas of Finland, has also changed lasts this season to produce narrower toe boxes and heels. This is good news to me personally as I use their product. Now I don't have to settle for a shorter boot to get the right width.

Choosing The Right System

The system you choose depends entirely on the type of skiing you want to pursue in the immediate future. If you are just a beginner, I certainly would not recommend the racing models. They are strictly for the experienced, well-seasoned skier.

I suggest that if your interest lies with in-track skiing, you should go with a "middle-of-the-road" touring system, that is, with skis that will function properly in machine-groomed, set tracks, as well as for off-track skiing. Then, after a couple of seasons of gaining experience, you might want to buy a light touring system or even a racing model system. Each individual's progress is different and is a direct result of several factors: natural athletic ability, determination, and time available for practice.

If possible, talk to other skiers and ask for their opinions on their own equipment. Check out the cross-country ski stores in your area and find one where the salespeople are experienced skiers. When I was just starting out I was fortunate to find such a retailer in Toronto. The name of the store is The Racing Stripe and I will be forever grateful to The Racing Stripe's knowledgeable salespeople's advice and guidance. Several of them are active racers who, through the trial-and-error method, have gained immense knowledge of the sport. As this outlet specializes in cross-country equipment, its personnel are in direct contact with all the major manufacturers who provide in-store demonstrations of their products.

Although it is difficult for most skiers to test equipment before spending their hard-earned dollars, some manufacturers are now selling to the cross-country skier through on-slope demos. At these demonstrations, companies such as Karhu allow you to use their boots, bindings, and skis at no charge. This is indeed a step in the right direction, and I am sure that this practice will become the norm as the "ski wars" heat up in future. It is also an advantage to belong to a ski club because you can try out the other skiers' equipment.

Rather than going into great detail about my own likes and dislikes, I will describe my own criteria for evaluating the various systems. Racing and touring are very different things (my greater interest lies in racing), and everything must be put into its proper perspective. To this end, it is necessary to use not one but two sets of criteria for evaluation purposes: one for performance (in-track, light systems, used for racing), and one for touring (out of track).

For me, a performance system must include boots that fit very well. Performance boots must feel light. Next comes the boot-to-binding connection. Is it tight enough? Does it have enough torsional rigidity on the turns and during downhills? Next check out the forward flexibility of the boot during the diagonal stride and the double-pole, single-kick movements.

Ideally it is best to ski some distance on a system. This way you can feel how the boots break over the tops of your toes and whether you will have metatarsal pains caused from a lack of support from the boots' soles.

As far as touring boots are concerned, fit is equally as important. Lightness, naturally, is not a critical factor; you are buying a higher-cut boot and it is bound to be a little heavier than a low-cut one. You certainly don't want to feel, however, that you are walking around with two cement blocks attached to your feet. It is very important that a touring boot gives good support off-track and is torsionally right for turning control.

These are my own criteria. In testing the various boot/binding systems I found all were good to ski on. The higher level of performance of all the new incompatible systems make the old compatibles almost obsolete in my opinion. These are the highlights of the various tests I conducted.

The Salomon SNS system to me is still the Rolls Royce of the cross-country world. It offers an unparalleled boot-to-binding link. The SNS binding flex-plate and D-ring tab eliminate excessive boot break over the toes, thereby considerably lessening the possibility of instep and toe problems.

Although I initially had foot problems with the SR90 boot—the heel plate tore up my own heel—the problem has been overcome. The SR901 and SR901 Equipe racing boots are a pleasure to wear. I was pleasantly surprised to find that both, although of very light construction and with less rigid soles, still provided excellent torsional support.

As far as the touring boots were concerned, I was most impressed with Merrell's (a Salomon licensee) Gore-Tex boots. Maybe I'm a little prejudiced here because of my previous inability to find a boot with a narrower last. Now at last somebody has given some thought to those people with skinny, bony feet.

These boots are indeed a pleasure to wear. The reduced rigidity of the soles will also be advantageous to skiers with a less developed technique.

The Contact system by Trak is more than adequate; in fact, in my opinion, it is almost the equal of the Salomon SNS system. The hinged housing on the binding is a real asset and, like the Salomon system, offers great freedom of movement during the kicking process while reducing excessive boot break over the toes. The boot-to-binding relationship is excellent as well. I was most impressed by the degree of control that I experienced while skating on the flats and around corners. The Ultra Light CS400 racing boot and the CS250 light touring boots are comfortable and rate at least an eight on a scale of one to ten. In summation, the Contact system is a smooth, slick, and efficient system.

For the tourer the CS100 boot and accompanying 202 binding is also impressive. The boot, although high-cut, is surprisingly light in weight and feels like a comfortable slipper when worn. Not only is it comfortable, but it offers excellent support and eliminates foot "fatigue" dramatically.

I want to emphasize that these are not the only systems you should consider. Other systems such as Nike, Trakker, and Lin are made by responsible and reliable companies. Each company has developed innovative equipment of great benefit to the sport. Nike, for example, through experience and expertise in the running-shoe business, has developed one of the most advanced and comfortable cross-country racing boots available.

Now that we have covered some of the sophisticated and advanced technological changes taking place, let's bring it all into proper perspective. I can best accomplish this by relating a story told to me by a fellow skier who is a member of the same ski club as I am.

My friend, who I am sure wishes to remain anonymous (you'll see why later on), was skiing by himself at a local conservation area when he met a gentleman in his sixties who was an obvious devotee of the sport of cross-country skiing. My friend asked the older man if he would care to join him in a "casual" tour around a marked ten-kilometer course. The stranger thought that this was a great idea and said that he welcomed the company. Allow me to describe the scene in greater detail. My friend, wearing a racing suit and outfitted in the latest boot/binding combo, was mounted on a pair of racing skis. In contrast, his newfound friend wore an old pair of dog-eared touring leather boots mounted on wide "antique" wooden skis. The man himself looked like an antique.

During the first time around the course, the two skiers bantered back and forth with bits of trite but polite conversation. At the conclusion of the first ten-kilometer loop both skiers decided that they would ski the second lap at a faster pace. To my friend's amazement the older skier took off like a jackrabbit, using the longest stride my friend has ever seen. The old guy was flying over the trail with my elegant friend in desperate pursuit. As each kilometer passed, the old veteran seemed to get stronger and stronger. At about the eight-kilometer mark, my friend's tongue was nearly dragging on the snow, and he was gasping for breath. He started to slip back from exhaustion, and at one point fell on a slight downhill section. The elderly man, sensing something was amiss, skied back to his companion and apologetically asked, "Am I going too fast for you?" My embarrassed friend replied that the pace was just fine and made up a feeble excuse about his wax not gripping properly and causing him to slip. The truth was that he was wasted, finished.

Needless to say, my skiing buddy declined the veteran's invitation to ski one more loop. Upon receiving a negative reply, the vet mentioned that he would be returning the next day and asked if my friend would care to join him. My friend declined the invitation by inventing another feeble excuse.

As he retreated to his car with his tail between his legs, the old fellow bounded down the trail once again in seemingly effortless fashion.

The moral of the story is obvious. Never judge a skier by the equipment he wears. It's how you use that equipment, however limited it may appear, that really counts. The next time you're shopping for the latest in cross-country ski equipment, don't get too carried away with all the glitter, glamour, and promises. Owning the greatest equipment in the world will not transform you into a good skier; you still have to pay your dues in practice time and training.

Poles

Shafts

Cross-country ski pole shafts can be separated into four categories according to what they're made of: tonkin (bamboo-like grass), fiberglass, aluminum alloys, and carbonfiber.

Tonkin is heated and treated for maximum flexibility. Over the years the bamboo tends to dry out and develop lengthwise cracks or splits, especially in drier climates. On the positive side, if tonkin poles are badly cracked or split during the course of an outing, they can be held together by electrician's tape and will at least get you home. The bamboo pole is generally inexpensive and well suited to the budget-minded skier or beginner.

Fiberglass is much stronger than tonkin and resists cracking. If fallen on or exposed to unusual stress, however, the shaft tends to break cleanly in two or shatter into irreparable slivers. Since manufacturers started to put spiral as well as longitudinal glass fibers in the shaft, the breakage problem has been greatly minimized.

The light aluminum alloys, introduced in the early 1970s, have proven to be very popular for light touring and touring in general. The aluminum pole is fairly light in weight, resists breakage extremely well, and will last for a lifetime with normal use.

The carbonfiber pole is an ultralight pole designed for the citizen racer who demands the best. Although it gives the appearance of being brittle, just the opposite is true. It will stand up to years of use. Carbonfiber poles are designed for in-track use only. They are not suited to off-track skiing due to their lack of flotation, meaning that when they are implanted in the snow they penetrate too deeply.

Baskets and Tips

Years ago, baskets were huge in circumference. They consisted of bamboo rings held together with strips of leather, which stretched out of shape or tore with wear and moisture.

Today, baskets are made of plastic mixed with vinyl and are of one-piece moulded construction. The greater the mixture of vinyl, the greater the basket's resistance to breakage in the cold.

Most baskets snap on or off for easy installation or replacement. Small-diameter models are used for in-track skiing, wider baskets for off-track touring.

Tips are made of hardened steel alloy or carbide alloys in order to last. You will notice that tips are angled forward. This facilitates the withdrawal of the poles from the snow.

Grips and Wrist Straps

Most of the the less expensive poles have grips made of plastic. The problem with plastic grips is that they tend to get slippery if snow or moisture collects on the handle. Plastic is also colder to handle compared with leather. Leather grips are easier to hold and will not slide from the glove in the semi-release motion made by the hand following the pole plant. Leather grips are usually found on the more expensive poles.

Wrist straps are made of either leather or woven nylon. Adjustable straps are of great benefit as they can be tightened or expanded to suit gloved or bare hands. Inexpensive poles tend to offer non-adjustable straps.

What's New in Poles?

The Swix company has brought aluminum poles back into the limelight with what they call an exercise skiing/citizen racing model called the Alu Light. Alu Lights are made with sixteen-millimeter thick high-strength (alloy 7075) aluminum shafts that are tapered for improved swing weight. The grips are made of cork and the wrist straps of nylon. The cup-shaped baskets are small and aerodynamic. The carbide tips are offset to give better bite on the snow.

Exel has revived their aluminum Final model by tapering the aluminum shafts and adding a "soft," cup-shaped basket with carbide tip. The leather grip is canted to conform with hand contours and has adjustable nylon straps.

Exel also has developed a thicker aluminum pole for general touring and back-country skiing called the Powder. The Powder features tapered shafts, all-leather grips with adjustable nylon straps and wide, round baskets for added support in deep off-track snow.

In the non-aluminum line, Swix has introduced a brand-new pole for serious racers. The ultralight Swix Light poles (each pole weighs 114 grams or 4 ounces) are the lightest competition poles on the market today. The shafts are carbonfiber that has been coated with epoxy resin, sanded smooth, and then lacquered for added strength and abrasion resistance. Swix Lights also feature cork grips, easy adjusting nylon straps, and aerodynamic baskets with offset carbide tips.

Decide exactly what type of skiing you will be doing before buying poles. There are poles for back-country, off-track skiing, poles for in-track light touring, poles for general touring, and poles for racing. What you choose is up to you.

When checking for proper pole length, stand with one arm out perpendicular to your side. Place the pole that you are testing under your armpit. Now drop your arm to your side. If the top of the pole doesn't touch your armpit, it is too short. The properly fitted pole fits snugly under your armpit without discomfort.

Clothing and Other Necessities

It is important to control your loss of body heat if you are on the trail for prolonged periods. Failure to do so could result in hypothermia (the body's inability to maintain an adequate temperature). One is insulated not by clothing, but by the air that is trapped within it. The layer of clothing next to the skin should be of a loose weave, therefore, to allow a layer of air to surround the body. Fishnet-style underclothing, or underwear woven to give a waffle pattern, are both good. Secondary layers of clothing (shirts and sweaters) must retain body heat while absorbing body moisture and transmitting it to the outside to evaporate. Since the weather may change continuously while you are skiing, you will have to control your body temperature by adding or removing clothing. Wear types of clothing that can be put on or taken off easily on the trail. You will need a wind-proof outer layer of clothing when it is windy or when you are skiing quickly on long downhills. You should also carry spare socks and inner gloves to change during the day. Wool socks are desirable, particularly if your feet perspire a great deal. Synthetic materials lose their insulating qualities when wet.

Snowsuits or snowmobile outfits are far too warm and are not suitable wear for adults. They may, however, be fine for young children who move very slowly during the learning stage. Since most heat loss occurs via the head, wear a toque.

Nordic Wear—1980s Style

Now that we have covered some of the basics as to why cross-country skiers require certain kinds of clothing and why they dress as they do, let's take a look at what is available. As I pointed out previously, all equipment purchased, including clothing, depends on the type of skiing you want to pursue. For example, the type of clothing purchased for back-country or wilderness skiing will vary greatly from that intended for light touring and racing. Back-country clothing includes knickers and an anorak (a lightweight shell parka, usually hooded). Racers wear a one-piece Lycra stretch suit.

If I were to detail all the clothing that is available today, I would have to write another book on the subject. I only intend to highlight trends and new developments in clothing. I myself dress in Lifa underwear with a track suit over the top. In extreme cold, I may add a wool sweater for added warmth. I guess I still adhere to my old "KISS" (Keep It Simple, Stupid) philosophy, and I'll probably never change. Most people seem to be a little more fashion-conscious than I am, however, so let's take a glimpse at what is available.

Let's start off with something spicy. How about silk underwear? It's expensive, but it works! It's available from Eddie Bauer, Early Winters, and LL Bean. Silk is a long-lasting, non-absorbent, breathing natural product.

Before you rush out to buy silk underwear, however, you should take a look at polypropylene. It is a hydrophobic fiber that transports body moisture away from the body while providing excellent insulation. One word of caution: don't throw polypropylene into hot water or the dryer as it will melt. For a warm, lightweight layer that will keep you dry, polypropylene is an excellent product. Manufacturers of polypropylene include Helly-Hansen, Patagonia, Wickers, and Royal Robbins.

Next, companies such as Protogs, James, and CB Sports are combining polypropylene with wool. The advantage of this combination is that not only does the polypropylene look after moisture transport, but the wool, which is on the outside, provides an extra thermal layer. This type of material is excellent for back-country skiing.

Another new development is the exclusive TRP underwear from Odlo. This material, knit from a polyester yarn, has a special rib construction that is supposed to provide superior air space and porosity. The yarn is non-absorbent and offers maximum transport of moisture from the body. One advantage that TRP underwear has over polypropylene is that it does not melt on contact with either hot water or a hot dryer.

Next on the agenda is the coming of age of powder suits. These powder suits are lightweight, allow for tremendous freedom of movement and, I must admit, look and feel good. These powder suits, which keep getting lighter every year, are made of polyester/cotton blends or tri-blends (poly/cotton and nylon) and are insulated with Thinsulate or Sontique. Powder suits can be worn over a sweater and underwear or can provide an outer layer of protection over a shell and pants. Another advantage is that powder suits don't emphasize the bulges you don't want anyone to see.

The final blow to the traditionalists—including my idol "Jack-rabbit" Smith-Johannsen, who will likely cringe in horror in his cabin—is the news of the extravagant colors and color combinations that are now available. Manufacturers such as Odlo and Colmar are offering colors and color combinations never seen before in the world of cross-country skiing. Colors such as lilac, cyclamen (a rosy red), ocher (mustard yellow), grappa (deep forest green), mauve, electric blue, copen (a lilac), edelweiss (a pale green), and lacquer red are now the "norm." In addition the manufacturers have taken it one step further and are now making hats and gloves in colors to match the outfits. Times and fashions change, but one thing seems to be here to stay—color. You have two alternatives as I see it: you can be good and colorful, or you can just be colorful. The choice is yours.

Last but not least, let's take a look at the availability of stretch clothing for the racer and the exhibitionist (those skiers with good physiques). Manufacturers such as Mother Lode, Helly-Hansen,

Odlo, Sunbuster, Colmar, and Terinit include the "miracle" fabric lycra—a super-stretchy material—in their fabrics because it adds a great deal of elasticity. To be efficient, racing suits need to be lightweight and feel like a second skin. Improved blends such as nylon/lycra or polyester/lycra are resulting in extremely light racing suits. Some are even constructed with a double nylon thickness in front for wind protection and only a single thickness in the back to keep the ounces down.

As far as the traditionalists are concerned, they can still purchase knickers or full-length stretch pants with the lycra fabric from companies such as Hind-Wells, Odlo, and Colmar.

Knickers continue to offer comfort and easy movement, as well as an effective layering system consisting of underwear, pullover sweater and vest, and anorak or parka. Body temperature can be regulated simply by adding or removing a layer as you warm up or cool down.

Other Rations
In addition to clothing, you must provide your body with extra liquids and energy foods. Carry both with you. Remember to bring your own liquid refreshments with you as the water in some ski areas is not fit to drink. It should be noted that alcoholic beverages cause the body to lose heat. Water is still the best liquid to take, along with raisins, nuts, or a granola bar. A fanny pack is ideal for carrying these rations and any extra clothing.

These necessities are a safeguard when skiing on a wilderness trail, or over long distances. If you are skiing at a resort with a five-kilometer or ten-kilometer loop leading back to the chalet, it is not necessary to carry everything with you. It is wise, however, to have extra clothing in your car or at the chalet just in case.

Chapter Two
Waxing

A NUMBER OF YEARS AGO, when I was participating in a masters cross-country ski championship, I came to realize that it is best to wax your own way and not to follow the leader. As the competitors gathered in the waxing area, most of the conversation, naturally, concerned the wax of the day. Some of the competitors had tried green wax in the −20° C (−5° F) temperature and said that it worked perfectly. Others said that hard blue wax was just as good. Still others were using mysterious wax combinations and making the whole process look like a Hollywood production number. A number of skiers were melting in a six-inch length of grip wax under the foot area while others were putting on an eighteen-inch length of grip wax.

In one corner of the room a quiet, bearded, and reserved man was seen dotting the "kick" area of his skis with red wax. "Red wax in −20° C temperatures? He's got to be kidding!" I said to myself. Several competitors, knowing who this man was, kept their thoughts to themselves. Others, not knowing his identity, almost laughed at the sight of this man placing tiny gobs of red wax on his skis.

The man they laughed at won the race in his age category. Incidentally he just happened to be a "legend" in Canadian cross-country skiing circles. Red wax for −20° C temperatures?

Absurd? I guess not. It worked for him, and who can knock success? Certainly not the losers. "The legend" probably broke all the rules of ski waxing, which would cause the wax manufacturers to throw up their hands in disbelief and frustration.

Remember, nobody is completely right and nobody is completely wrong when it comes to waxing. Individuals must experiment and use and re-use what works best for them. There are some commonsense rules to follow, however, that offer logical reasons why you should use certain waxes for specific snow conditions. Getting back to "the legend": nobody knew what he had used as a base wax. Obviously he had still followed the basics to a point and had then simply improvised. His skis gripped the snow at the point of his "kick" contact with the snow. The end result is what counts.

Let's take a brief look at why and how certain hard and soft waxes work under various snow conditions. Basically the shape of the snow crystals dictates the type of wax to be used. For example, a freshly fallen cold powder snow crystal has long spikes reaching out from its center. The spikes, which are sharp, jab into the wax on the base of the ski. Because they are so sharp, a hard wax is all that is needed for grip.

As the new snow crystals warm up and melt, the sharp spikes become dull and slanted; you therefore need stickier or softer wax to grip these shorter spikes.

When the snow becomes old in the form of soft slush, ice, or crust, it is no longer in crystal form. The spikes disappear, leaving the round centers. Now, you need extremely sticky waxes or klisters to grip these remaining centers.

I have tried to simplify waxing for you by dividing it into two separate categories: simple and progressive.

Simple Waxing

To become proficient in the art of waxing takes a lot of practice—like skiing itself. It is always easier to wax for colder conditions, i.e., −4° C to −10° C (14° F to 27° F). Usually the temperatures in most skiing areas are in this temperature range during the months of December and January and in early February. In these temperatures you can experiment with the green and blue waxes, or a combination of both. Before we get into the application of the different waxes, we'll take a look at the equipment you need to apply the wax properly.

Scrapers. I have always felt that metal scrapers do the best job in removing old wax from the skis' surface. There are some claims that plastic or acrylic scrapers are easier on ski bases. Wax remover spray or liquid is essential as well.

Waxing corks. I would recommend that you carry two separate corks. A synthetic cork is ideal for smoothing on klister waxes or basebinder wax. Natural corks are best for use on hard waxes such as green and blue. The two-cork system also prevents the blending of extremely soft klisters with harder waxes.

Heating equipment for application. As propane works better than butane in cold temperatures, I recommend that you purchase a propane bottle and attachable torch as well as a waxing iron. The waxing iron is not large like a clothes iron as some people think, but is very compact with a handle.

Other accessories. Once you have acquired all the basic tools to do the job properly, you may wish to add a few frills. I call them frills because they are not really necessary at the outset, in my opinion. A few of the extras include a waxing block, a groove scraper, a portable waxing table, a thermometer, a sanding block, and epoxy repair compound.

Waxes

Over the years, I have tried many different brands from several manufacturers. Personally, I prefer Swix waxes. They are easy to apply and have proven to be the most reliable. As far as klisters are concerned, I do, however, prefer the Jackrabbit klisters: one for dry and one for wet conditions.

The following chart shows the types of grip waxes that I would buy to get started and the temperatures at which they work best under specific snow conditions. Before we look at the chart, I should add that it is of great benefit to purchase "binder" wax. Binder wax accomplishes just what its name indicates. It prepares your base so that any wax you apply will adhere to the base for a longer period of time. Orange Basebinder is excellent for this purpose.

The important thing about waxing is to remember what works for you. If necessary, write down the snow conditions, temper-

WAXING CHART

Wax	Temperature	Snow Conditions
Polar	Below −22° C (Below 10° F)	Powder
Green	−22° C to −8° C (10° F to 16° F)	Powder
Blue	−7° C to −2° C (19° F to 27° F)	Powder
Violet	0° C (32° F)	Powder to wet
Red	1° C to 2° C (34° F to 36° F)	Wet
Yellow	2° C to 3° C (36° F to 38° F)	Very Wet

Note: If you are not satisfied with the red and yellow, try Jackrabbit wet. For icy, crusty snow below 0° C (32° F) I recommend Jackrabbit dry.

Glider Waxes (for tips and tails only)

Green	Below −10° C (Below 14° F)	
Blue	−10° C to −5° C (14° F to 23° F)	
Violet	−5° C to +3° C (23° F to 37° F)	

ature, etc. at the end of the day so that you can refresh your memory. Don't rely on wax charts to be infallible because there are simply too many variables.

The Variables

Ski camber. The skis themselves sometimes dictate what wax to use under certain conditions. Generally speaking, if the camber of the ski is fairly stiff, you may have to use the next softest wax. For example, if the temperature and conditions call for green wax and you are slipping back when executing the kick, you may have to drop down to blue.

The skier's technique. Some skiers with excellent technique may be able to get away with using a harder wax because they are able to "weight down" the ski with a little extra effort. They are physically able to adjust their technique slightly if at first they don't weight down enough. This, of course, requires great concentration and technique.

Other skiers, whose technique is only adequate and who have limited experience, are unable to exert enough weighting down onto the kicking ski. These skiers should add a softer wax to obtain the necessary grip for kicking purposes.

Types of ski. It has always been my experience that wooden skis must be waxed softer than fiberglass skis. If, for example, temperatures call for blue wax, I would probably use blue wax as a base first on wooden skis, but would place a violet "kicker" on top of it. Under the same conditions, if the skier using the wooden skis were a relative beginner, I would wax the skis with violet. The wax would be applied from a point six to eight inches from the tails. The logic for the two different methods lies in the fact that one skier has good technique while the other does not. The beginner's wax must be softer or stickier because he lacks expertise in weighting and unweighting (or weight transfer).

The Waxing Process

Let's proceed on the premise that you are waxing for blue-to-green temperature conditions. If you are fairly certain that the temperatures forecasted for the next day are reasonably accurate, then you can wax the night before. I hate to lose valuable time when I arrive at the trails after an hour's drive, by spending still another hour waxing skis. It's such a pleasure to be able to get out of the car, do some stretching exercises, and then take off along the trails. On a very few occasions, my selection of wax the night before has been incorrect and I have had to wax again. That's life, however, and you just have to make adjustments.

Glide waxing. Take your blue glider wax and touch it to a hot iron while holding it close to the ski's surface. Remember you're only using the glider wax for tips and tails. Let the hot wax drip on to the ski's surface—six to eight inches from both ends of the skis—making sure to cover the entire width of the ski. Wax either tips or tails first. Take the hot iron and melt in the drippings. Make sure that you have as uniform and as smooth an application as possible. Once you have applied the glider wax to both skis take your metal scraper and gently scrape it over the wax on the ski you finished first. This will smooth out the surface and remove protruding lumps. Repeat this procedure with the other ski. You have now completed the glide wax portion.

Applying basebinder wax. The orange basebind should be hot-waxed onto the ski base and warmed using a waxing iron as well. The basebinder should cover the area between the glide-waxed areas. Let it cool, then polish it smooth using the synthetic cork. As previously mentioned, be cautioned against using the same cork for your final wax preparation. Using the cork that contains sticky particles of basebinder wax on final waxes will dramatically reduce the effectiveness of the wax of the day. Leave the skis outside for an hour or so before applying the wax of the day.

Final wax application. Now that you're finally ready to complete your waxing masterpiece, one final decision has to be made. I mentioned earlier that we were going to wax for blue-to-green temperature conditions. In other words, the wax of the day could be either green or blue. If bright sunshine is expected, it is inevitable that the snow temperature will rise as the day progresses.

First, apply the harder wax—in this case, green—in liberal amounts on the kicking area (between the glide-to-glide area) on each ski. Using a hot waxing iron, melt in the green wax. Then smooth in the wax with a "natural" cork. Leave it for a few minutes and put on a second, lighter layer of green. Cork the wax into the ski as before. It is neither necessary nor wise to use the waxing iron for the second layer.

The next application of wax will be with the blue wax. The only difference in application from the green is that you should reduce the length of the waxing surface by six to eight inches at both the tips and tails. Repeat with a second layer of blue wax, and cork it into the surface.

The final test. Upon arrival at the resort, try out your wax on the flats and on slight inclines. If it is very early in the morning, you may find that you have excellent grip, but lack a little something in the glide. I wouldn't worry about this. As snow temperatures rise, that blue wax should work to perfection. Always remember, it is best to wax for grip rather than slip.

Should the temperature rise due to an unexpected warm front moving in, you might find that your skis are slipping back and that grip is non-existent. This is no problem. Reach for your violet wax and apply it on the top of the existing waxes in the kick area. Sound simple? It is simple, if you apply waxes in order of their hardness—hardest to softest.

Progressive Waxing Techniques

During the past decade, the wax manufacturers, through thousands of hours of dedicated research, have developed new waxes designed to increase your speed by fractions of seconds. As competition became keener and keener, those fractions of a second became the difference between winning the gold medal and winning the silver medal. The straight blue wax wasn't good enough anymore, so a second blue wax was invented for snow temperatures between −17° C and −5° C (0° F and 22° F) called Blue Extra. Then came another blue with a green mix called Blue Special for −6° C to −4° C (21° F to 25° F). There is also a Special Green designed to cover −15° C to −10° C (5° F to 14° F), and an extra blue with a violet mix in it for temperatures ranging from −2° C to 0° C (28° F to 32° F).

Confused, bewildered, and perplexed? I know how you feel because I went through it. Actually, though, most tourers and citizen racers find, through experimentation, that most of the extra and special waxes are ideal for local conditions, wherever that might be. I think they work better than the straight blues, greens, etc.

If you are skiing in other areas within your own country where humidity levels may vary substantially, it is wise to carry a few waxes from several manufacturers such as Rode, Vola, Toko, and Fall Line. In foreign countries, my policy would be to do as the locals do. My logic here is that the local manufacturers, through on-snow trials and tribulations, have developed specific waxes for specific snow conditions. They, above anyone else, should know what waxes to use in their own climate.

If there is one thing that I have learned about waxing over the years, it is that practical experience is the best teacher. I'll never forget my first cross-country race, when I was told that a particular wax was the only one to use. I took the advice and lived to regret it. Each step forward was followed by three steps backward. I was being passed with ease by pre-teen skiers as if I were standing still. I vowed from that day on that I would "do my own thing" when it came to waxing, and I have stood by that philosophy ever since.

As of the writing of this book, I see the art of waxing becoming even more complicated as the manufacturers scramble for

increased market share. On the other hand, the same manufacturers are also spending a great percentage of their research time
developing the perfect two-wax system for weekend skiers—the
average tourer.

Who knows? Maybe some day one wax will be invented with
chemical properties that will adjust to every conceivable snow
condition. Sounds like a dream doesn't it? It will probably happen, but not in my lifetime.

In conclusion I want to emphasize that even perfect waxing
will not transform you from a mediocre skier into an expert. That
transformation only comes about through hours and hours of
dedicated practice in technique along with specific emphasis on
conditioning and training.

I have, by design, avoided giving you complicated wax charts,
dotted with asterisks indicating numerous snow conditions where
several waxes could be used. As far as I am concerned, this
would be an exercise in futility. I have, however, assembled a
table of waxes listed according to their degree of hardness as a
helpful guide in selecting the wax or waxes of the day.

RELATIVE HARDNESS TABLE

Wax	Hardness
Polar	4500 hard
Green Special	4100
Green	3100
Green Extra	2700
Blue Special	1900
Blue	1400
Blue Extra	600
Violet Special	350
Violet	140
Red Special	120
Red	110
Red Extra	105
Yellow Klister	100 soft

Chapter Three
Training

FITNESS IN ANY SPORT does not occur without some effort on the part of the participant. Cross-country skiing is no exception. Training, meaning a planned exercise program, is most important in preparing for the season ahead. See your doctor before starting any conditioning program.

Since most people are not preparing for the next Olympic Games, I do not feel that an intense training program is necessary. I do feel strongly, though, that some physical conditioning is essential before taking up any sport. I recommend a two-phase program. Phase one firms the body and phase two develops cardiovascular fitness. They should be used together for overall conditioning. Plan to exercise early in the morning, or at night, a minimum of three times weekly. Don't worry about what you are like now. Don't let your age or present physical condition discourage you. Start slowly, building gradually.

Firming Up

Sit-ups. To strengthen the abdominal muscles, lie on your back on the floor with knees bent slightly and hands behind the neck. Now raise your upper body up and touch your knees with your elbows. If this is too difficult at first, tuck your feet under a suitable object. Try to do ten sit-ups at a time (you may only be able to do five in the beginning). Increase the number by one or two each workout, until you work up to thirty or more.

Push-ups. These are excellent for developing your shoulders, chest, and arms. Upper body strength is important in cross-country skiing as poling, particularly double poling, is very demanding. Lie flat on your stomach, with your hands palm down on each side of your chest. Keeping your body straight, raise yourself up to a straight-arm position, using either your toes or your knees (using the knees is less strenuous) as the base of the angle. Lower yourself back down so that your chest almost touches the floor and repeat. Do as many repetitions as you can manage and try to increase the number from workout to workout until you are able to do more than thirty push-ups.

Groin exercise. Sit on the floor. Bring both feet up so that the soles of your feet are touching one another. With both hands clasped around your feet, lean forward, keeping your back flat, and hold for five seconds. Repeat six times. You will be glad you stayed with this one after the first ski of the season!

Half squats. To firm up thigh muscles, stand with your feet eight inches apart and with your heels elevated one or two inches on a thick book. Place a broomstick behind your head and across your shoulders. Now bend your legs slowly until you are almost in a sitting position. Hold this position for two seconds, then slowly return to a standing position. Repeat six to ten times. Add one or two repetitions each workout until you reach over thirty. An even more effective way to get the maximum results from this exercise is to replace the broomstick with a light barbell.

Cardiovascular Fitness

Cardiovascular fitness is determined by the ability of the cardio-respiratory system to transport oxygen from the lungs to the working muscles. Training to improve cardiovascular fitness increases the capacity of the body to use oxygen by strengthening the respiratory muscles, thereby improving the pumping efficiency of the heart and the quality and quantity of the blood. Cardiovascular fitness training also increases endurance—the length of time for which such work can be continued.

The most important and only investment you will have to make initially is the purchase of good-quality running shoes. Look for shoes with good cushioning in the heel area. This allows the heel to absorb the shock of hitting the ground and will help prevent leg and foot injuries.

Start with a warm-up to prevent injuries such as pulled muscles and other running-related injuries:

1) Put both hands on a wall at shoulder height and lean forward. Extend one leg in a straight position behind you with the heel touching the floor. With the foot of that leg start to exert some pressure as if you were pushing an object. Repeat six or more times until you can feel some stretching of the muscles in the back of the leg. Alternate legs. This exercise helps to prevent hamstring muscle injuries.

2) Another excellent stretching movement is to place one leg at a time on the back of a chair or other solid object at about waist level. Slowly lean forward, keeping your back flat, until you feel some stretching of the muscles in your leg. Repeat six or more times and alternate legs.

3) Strike the same pose as in the last exercise, except that instead of leaning forward, rock slightly backwards on the stationary foot. This is an excellent exercise for the inside thigh muscle.

4) The famous Achilles heel injury has brought about the demise of many a great athlete's career. It is most important to stretch this area before starting a workout. Simply stand with both feet on a step as you face up the stairs. The balls of your feet should be on the edge of the stairs, your heels protruding over the edge. Now raise and lower your heels slowly using the front of your feet for leverage. This exercise can be performed on any elevated surface. Repeat ten to twelve times.

To Run or Not to Run: An Important Decision
Not all people are meant to be runners. A physical deformity or an old injury may prevent many people from running. There are many other means of achieving cardiovascular fitness in preparation for cross-country skiing, such as striding, roller skiing, swimming, and cycling.

Regardless of which means of conditioning you choose, you should first familiarize yourself with heart rates, because they indicate your physical condition and should be used to monitor your performance and physical well-being.

To find your training heart rate, you must first find your resting heart rate and your maximum heart rate. Here are simple methods of figuring out your heart rates. To find your resting heart rate, place the index and middle finger on your wrist and count your pulse for thirty seconds. Multiply the number of beats by two to get the number of beats per minute, or your resting pulse. To calculate your maximum heart rate, subtract your age from 220. (An individual's maximum heart rate drops with age.) To establish your training heart rate, use this formula: maximum heart rate *minus* resting pulse *times* 65 percent *plus* resting pulse *equals* training rate.

The training rate is what you need to work with to improve cardiovascular conditioning. You should be working at or above your training rate. As the intensity of your workouts will vary, I advise you to train in a range from 60 percent to 90 percent of your maximum heart rate.

Running: Train, Don't Strain!
Start out slowly on a measured course. You may want to measure the distance around the block where you live if you are running outdoors. After completing one or two laps, you might want to call it a day. Don't push yourself to the exhaustion point. When you feel fatigued, slow down and walk or jog slowly back to the starting point. Cool down, do some stretching exercises, and call it a day. Set a realistic goal for yourself. For example, if you have run a one-kilometer course for two weeks, try to run a two-kilometer course for the next two weeks. Remember, only you know your limitations.

Don't worry about your time. Over the years I have seen too many people give up on a running program because they have become obsessed with the stopwatch. Remember, you are running for fun, for cardiovascular conditioning, and for your own satisfaction. During the first few months, your goal should be to complete a two-, five-, or even ten-kilometer run, depending on your individual conditioning. Later you might want to time yourself in order to find out your per-kilometer pace. You can set new goals as time passes. The same principles apply to striding, cycling, or roller skiing.

Striding

If you have not been active for a number of years, I think it wise to start out by "striding." Striding is basically the same movement as walking but with longer-than-normal steps. Striding is achieved by placing greater emphasis on the "push off" foot to lengthen the normal stride. Striding can be maintained by accentuating the arm action. Let both arms swing freely so that they are perpendicular to your body. A good arm swing will automatically help propel the legs and will enable you to maintain a good brisk pace. Measure off a course that is not too demanding and gradually increase your daily distance over a four- to six-week period, until you have worked up to a thirty- to forty-minute workout. At the end of this time period you may want to start a running program. Before doing so, however, you should recheck your heart rate.

Roller Skiing, Roller Skating, and Training Gadgets

You may wish to supplement a running or cycling and swimming program with roller ski training. Roller skiing closely resembles snow skiing except that it is done on pavement. Wheels take the place of snow and allow you to simulate cross-country skiing techniques. Some skiers alternate running and roller skiing. If you feel that running is not for you, then you may wish to concentrate on roller skiing for cardiovascular conditioning.

Roller skis are becoming more sophisticated each year, although the perfect roller ski has yet to be invented. I like the two-wheel roller skis, which allow you to control your speed by "snowplowing." Roller skiing comes closer to simulating real skiing than any other exercise. The two-wheel variety allows you to practise the marathon skate as well as the diagonal stride. The gliding quality is also excellent for an honest "double poling" workout.

There are at least six models of roller skis from which to

choose. I've tested Swede Ski, Exel, and Roleto. All have a different feel; some have three wheels (two wheels on the back, one on the front); others have two (one in front, one in back). I chose the Swede Ski (a two-wheeler) and have been very satisfied. I enjoy the skating technique and find that my two-wheeler skis are ideally suited to this technique. I can angle each ski in the same manner that I would angle the inside edges on regular cross-country skis. I also practise my double poling and diagonal stride on the same roller skis.

If you are interested only in practising your diagonal stride and double poling techniques then the three-wheeler skis are for you. Remember, though, you won't be able to truly simulate the skating technique because the three wheels don't angle enough to allow for a proper skating stance.

The basket, including the tips on your regular poles, should be removed and replaced for the summer with carbide tips. These extra-hard tips will be better able to penetrate the asphalt, thereby preventing slippage. The total cost for roller skis, carbide tips, and bindings is approximately $250. The wheels are usually good for about one thousand kilometers and can be replaced.

It takes at least two hundred kilometers of training to get the feel for your roller skis. Build your workouts gradually and be patient. Approximately 70 percent of your "normal" roller ski workout should consist of double poling, 15 percent will be skating and 15 percent diagonal striding. These percentages can be altered if you want to work on certain specific weaknesses. Diagonal striding can best be practised on gradual inclines. Repetitions on the same hill do wonders for your stamina. Be cautioned, however, against roller skiing down steep hills as stopping is extremely difficult at medium to fast speeds.

There is always something new coming on the market that changes training methods. The newest trend to hit the marketplace is the roller skate. It is a hockey skate featuring one row of wheels on an ice-skate boot. They have proven so effective that many National Hockey League teams now use them for training purposes in the off-season.

The advent of the roller skate could not have been more timely, because the top cross-country ski racers now employ the skating techniques most of the time for both short- and long-distance races. It is an exhausting technique to use continuously and requires a tremendous amount of training to build up the necessary strength and stamina.

If you decide to buy a pair of roller skates, it is recommended that you still use poles with them to simulate cross-country skiing. If I had to choose between roller skis and roller skates I would still choose the skis, as the movement and weight of the skis is closer to the real thing. Don't forget, it is also important to maintain that fine coordination between skis and poles in the off-season.

Another development in the wizardry department is the Sport Tester. It is used to measure your exercise effectiveness. It monitors your heart rate during both short-interval training workouts and long-distance training runs. It is very effective for those who want to keep long-distance workouts within certain limits of stress. It can be set like an alarm clock to emit a beep when your pulse reaches a certain preset speed. The Sport Tester also functions as a stopwatch. It is a worthwhile gadget to have in that it can help you to record your progress accurately.

The Nordic Track is a fitness machine that can be used to improve cardiovascular fitness. It is, as the name implies, designed for cross-country skiers. The feet kick and glide in a track on rolling foot pads. Poling action is achieved by pulling on the handles of spring-loaded ropes. It provides a good workout.

These sophisticated and revolutionary inventions can assist any athlete in any athletic endeavor. I would like to emphasize, however, that they shouldn't and can't replace the old-fashioned blood, sweat, and tears training methods. They can be used with some benefit in conjunction with hill training, weight lifting, roller skiing, and, of course, on-snow training during the winter. A regular training regimen and consistent daily exercise will ensure that you reach and maintain a satisfactory fitness level.

Your First Times Out on the Trail

During the first few times out on your skis, concentrate on getting used to the feel of them on your feet. I would suggest that you go to a golf course or park. Let the experience be fun and relaxed. Ski down a few gentle slopes. Do some hill climbing, even if it seems to be difficult at first. Most important, "walk" on your skis for as long as you can. Skiing is just like walking; it uses the same alternate arm and leg movement.

Don't give up, even though you may find it a struggle at first. Perseverance is the key to success. Experiment with your waxing by reading the waxing charts and application directions. Wax for grip; that is, find the wax for that particular day, one that will allow you to kick or lead off on one ski without constantly slipping back on your skis. Then you will have won half the battle.

Let The Youngsters Do Their Thing

Young children have a natural enthusiasm for any sport. Don't discourage them. Once they start out, let them go down any hill and take their falls. Youngsters naturally like the downhill aspect of the sport. That's fine because they will also learn to climb as well. Although it may seem cruel, don't help them get up from every fall. The best way to learn is through practical experience. Youngsters are better for the struggle if they learn for themselves how to maneuver both poles and skis. Plenty of encouragement and praise is, of course, most helpful, at all times.

Where To Develop Your Skiing Ability

You've been on your skis a few times and now you're ready for bigger and better things. I would suggest that you choose a ski area with groomed trails. That is a resort where a track setter is used to preset tracks. It is much easier to learn how to ski properly when you don't have to make your own trail. Many resorts have a beginners' trail of approximately two kilometers with gentle terrain. Start here and work your way up to the other trails gradually.

Trail Etiquette

Whether you are a novice cross-country skier or a racing hotshot, trail etiquette can make or break a day's pleasure on the trail. Often the inconsiderate action of one skier is enough to shake your faith in mankind and leave you depressed for the day. Lack of trail etiquette not only inconveniences others but can lead to serious injury. Here are some commonsense guidelines to follow, which make for safe, happy skiing for all.

1) *Don't park on the trail.* If you stop to add or remove clothing, make equipment adjustments, or take pictures, step off the trail so that other skiers will not have to detour around you. This is especially important on blind corners or downhill stretches of trail.

2) *Don't "hog" both tracks when skiing with a friend.* On one-way double-tracked trails nothing is more annoying than coming across two slow-moving skiers tying up both tracks, engaged in idle conversation.

3) *Watch your poles when passing.* Make a special effort when passing to tuck your poles out of the way. Follow-through when double poling is great, but not when it endangers an overtaken skier.

4) *Show patience when overtaking a slower skier.* It is nerve-racking when a fast skier waits until he is five feet behind a slow skier and then gives forth the Tarzan yell: "Track!" Not only is the slower skier overtaken, he is overcome with shock. Give notice well ahead of time.

5) *Lend assistance when needed.* If a skier is struggling, slipping back on his or her skis, offer encouragement, advice, or waxing assistance. You should always stop if a skier seems to be injured or has serious equipment problems. Don't forget, one good turn deserves another. Who knows, maybe one day the skier you helped will some day come to your assistance.

6) *Skiers going downhill have the right of way.* It's much easier for a skier going uphill to step off the trail, particularly in tight quarters, than it is for the faster skier heading down.

7) *Don't walk on the track.* Walking on trails, especially in soft snow, destroys them.

8) *Keep dogs off the trail.* This rule applies particularly to conservation areas where people hike with their dogs. Large dogs especially can damage a trail to the point of making skiing for any following individuals very unpleasant. There is nothing worse than having to remove brown klister from your skis.

9) *Don't be a track hog.* If another skier catches up to you on a single trail, have the courtesy to step off the trail rather than forcing them to pass on the unbroken snow beside the trail.

10) *Don't ski over your head.* If a particular trail has downhills that you know are too steep for your skiing ability, stay off them. Not only will you cause a logjam but your inconsiderateness could pose a danger both to you and to other skiers.

11) *When you fall, get off the trail.* Should you fall on a downhill section, remove your skis and as much of your body from the trail as is physically possible in order to let other skiers directly behind you pass safely.

12) *Ski in the indicated direction and observe all signs.* Many trails are marked as being one-way only.

13) *Don't litter!* If you pack it in, pack it out! Respect private property by closing gates and leaving fences intact, too.

Part Two
Mastering Ski Skills

How to Develop Your Technique
• Telemarking •
Non-Competitive Touring •
Cross-Country Skiing
for Seniors

The important thing to remember when learning technique is to enjoy your surroundings and have fun. Don't worry about the other skiers around you, some of whom may enjoy laughing at your expense. Chances are they can't do what you are attempting to do and are afraid to try. As nobody can master every technique overnight, repetition is the key to success.

To become proficient at certain turns and maneuvers, I recommend that you spend ten to fifteen minutes each time out on a hill where you can practise in peace and tranquility. By so doing, you will gain some confidence, which will help you enjoy your run on the trails that much more. Remember, practice makes perfect, and you will improve with each outing. I still spend a great deal of time at the outset of the season and during the season honing my skills by climbing up and skiing down the same hill. This way I get a feeling for my skis and improve my conditioning at the same time. This exercise will also afford you the opportunity to work on your weaknesses. For example, I have a tendency automatically to make right-hand turns wherever possible. I have to force myself to practise left-hand turns in order to become proficient at both.

Another method of self-improvement is to watch other skiers. If they appear proficient at a certain maneuver, don't be shy about asking for advice. Skiers are the friendliest people in the world, and their egos receive a boost when a stranger asks for advice.

When you have mastered some of the basic techniques, you may want to take part in a non-competitive tour. By so doing, you will be better able to test your learning experiences on a trail, perhaps one with which you are not familiar. I caution you, however, not to put pressure on yourself to excel in your first tour. Enjoy the surroundings and concentrate on what you have learned and how you can improve.

If adventure in cross-country skiing is what you are looking for, refer to Chapter Twelve, Where to Ski In Canada. This guide, compiled over the years, lists hundreds of ski areas and resorts. Its concise and easy-to-read format allows you to choose the right area for you, whether it be a ski weekend or the vacation of a lifetime you're after. Wherever you live in Canada, there is a ski area near you where you can enjoy Canada's fastest-growing winter sport.

Chapter Four

How To Develop Your Technique

IF YOU HAVE AN ATHLETIC BACKGROUND, you will probably be able to teach yourself to become proficient at the sport. This type of individual learns by watching others, by reading articles on technique, and by dedication. For most people, however, it is probably best to seek out a qualified instructor and get off to a proper start. Either way, the secret to success is practice, practice, and more practice.

Skiing Downhill

When going downhill, place your feet four to six inches apart. Keep your hips directly over your feet. Bend your knees slightly and lean forward with most of your weight on the balls of your feet. Your heels should be lightly resting on your skis. Your arms should be bent at the elbows away from your body. Your poles should be extended slightly behind your feet. The important thing to remember is—*relax*. Take a deep breath and let your skis "run." Avoid hesitation and continue to lean forward in the downhill position until you come to a complete stop.

Diagonal Stride

Diagonal Stride

The diagonal stride is similar to walking, only with a more fluid, gliding motion. It is the single most important technique that you will learn and is the main means of propelling your body forward. Practise the following using your poles for balance only.

With the back straight and the body at a 15° angle, put your weight on the ski that you intend to use to "push off." This is your "kicking" ski. With the leg bent slightly at the knee push off and straighten that leg. Now transfer your weight to the opposite ski and glide on that ski. Just as the glide ends, your glide ski now becomes your kicking ski. The other ski will now be the gliding ski. This is the kick-and-glide method—a process to be repeated over and over again.

How to get the rhythm. The secret of the kick-and-glide process is "weighting" and "unweighting." Just like walking on a trampoline, the weight is transferred from one foot to the other. When practising this weighting and unweighting process, don't be afraid to exaggerate. In other words, bend the leg at the knee as low as possible and spring upwards straightening the leg (just as you would on a trampoline). Shorten your glide, shift your weight to the gliding ski, and repeat the kick with the opposite ski. Fast repetitions are best as you will achieve a sense of rhythm more rapidly. As the weighting and unweighting process becomes second nature you can then think about lengthening your glide. Incidentally, this fast weight transfer exercise will stand you in good stead when it comes to climbing slight inclines.

Coordinating poling with diagonal stride. The proper use of your poles will not only assist you with the diagonal stride but will increase your forward thrust and speed considerably.

Each planting of the pole should coincide with the kicking ski. The pole should be planted on the same side as the gliding ski

at a point a few inches ahead of the boot on the kicking ski. Apply downward and backward pressure until the arm is fully extended back, then open the palm of the hand to relax. The arms should swing in a pendulum action.

Variations on the Diagonal Stride

Double pole, single kick method. As experience is gained you may wish to employ the double pole, single kick technique to relieve fatigue, or to initiate a change of pace. This method differs from the normal poling/kicking action in that you plant both poles in the snow when the kick takes place. At the end of the glide, the process is repeated using the same kicking ski over and over again. As your technique becomes more proficient and coordination improves, you may want to alternate the kicking ski from time to time.

Double poling only. This technique refers to the use of the poles only to provide propulsion. With the skis side by side, the poles are planted a few inches in front of the feet. Downward and backward pressure is exerted on the poles until the arms are fully extended behind the rest of the body. While the trunk or upper body may sometimes be almost parallel to the skis, it is vital to keep the head upright so that you are always looking straight ahead.

As you can imagine, double poling for a prolonged period of time requires tremendous upper body strength. This is achieved only with a rigorous training program. The serious racers, or "elite" cross-country skiers, rely to a great extent on double poling. They tend to wax for glide more than the average tourer and use a very small area of the ski's surface (just under the foot) for "kicking" wax.

Racers confronted with a slight upgrade, who find that double poling is ineffective, may switch to the diagonal stride. As very little kicking wax is used, weighting and unweighting becomes critical. Racers must depend on superior leg strength and timing to carry them through this stretch of the course.

Skating Techniques

The skating technique used in cross-country skiing is basically the same as in ice skating, although skating on skis is naturally more awkward because of the length of the skis. There are two skating methods used in skiing which I will refer to as the "full skate" and the "half skate."

Full skating method. This method is employed on the flats where there are no set tracks. To initiate the skating technique, put your weight on the inside edge of one ski and push off to one side (whichever side feels most comfortable). You can use both poles at once to help you gain momentum at the moment of push off. Lift the other ski and place it on the snow at a 45° angle to the push-off ski. Make sure the tail of this ski is ahead of and clear of the push-off ski.

Now transfer your full weight from the push-off ski to the gliding ski. As the glide ends, the gliding ski becomes the push-off ski and the process is repeated. Keep your body erect during the skating process, and lean forward slightly. Be careful to keep the poles clear of both skis while skating. As your balance and confidence in skating improves, you should eventually be able to hold both poles behind your back with your hands together. This is the "classic" skating technique.

Skating

Half skate or marathon skate. This method of skating is used while skiing on pre-set tracks and requires considerable leg strength. The half skate method is similar to that of the full skate, except that the "glide" ski always remains in the track. Put the push-off ski on the snow at a 45° angle outside the track. Transfer your weight to the push-off ski. Once you have pushed off, transfer your weight to the glide ski. Just as the glide ends, transfer your weight again to the push-off ski and repeat the process. Remember, the glide ski always remains in the tracks. I would advise all skiers to practise alternating the gliding leg and the push-off leg as the half skate is extremely strenuous.

At the moment when push off occurs, use double poling to generate added power and speed. Timing, practice, coordination, and patience are all required to perfect your technique. Once you have mastered skating, however, you will be amazed at the speed you can achieve and maintain over a prolonged period of time.

Slowing Down and Stopping

The most common and simplest method used to slow down or stop is the "snowplow." As the name implies, your skis form an inverted V—the tips of your skis are a few inches apart while

Snowplow

the tails are considerably farther apart. The larger you make the V, the more your speed will be reduced. The secret to making the snowplow work is inside "edging." The speed is dictated by how much pressure you place on the inside edges of both skis against the snow. Find a fairly well packed slope and practise the snowplow until you are able to regulate your speed consistently.

Falling and Getting Up After a Fall

Try to fall relaxed, to the side and backwards, so you land in soft snow, not on hard skis. It is quite normal to fall frequently when learning how to ski down hills. It is very important, therefore, for a skier to learn how to get up the easy way. These steps should be taken:

1) Remove the pole straps from your wrists.
2) While still lying on your side, bring your skis around so that they are parallel to one another. If your skis are tangled, roll onto your back so that both skis are in the air over your body. Swing them so that they are parallel to one another and across the slope below your body and lower them into the snow at right angles to the fall line.
3) Bend your knees so that the skis are brought under the body as close as possible.
4) Dig the inner edge of the downhill ski and the outer edge of the uphill ski into the snow.
5) Grasp both poles so that they are next to each other and can act as a single pole. Place the ski pole tips uphill in the snow about a foot from your knees. Grasp the poles just above the baskets with one hand. Place the other hand halfway up the shafts. Now you can push yourself up into a sitting position or onto your knees, and then up into a standing position. Always remember that the skis must be parallel to the side of the hill. If the skis are not parallel to the side of the hill, they will slide downhill as the skier gets up. This usually results in another fall and the skier has to start the process all over again.

Turning

After you have mastered the snowplow technique, the next step is to learn how to turn. I find that the ''wind-up and unwind'' method works best in teaching turning techniques.

Let's assume that you want to make a right-hand turn. As you near the spot where you want to turn, go into the snowplow position. When you want to turn, rotate your upper body and arms to the left. Keep your head straight ahead and continue to look downhill. Your right arm is now ahead and in front of your body. This is the ''wind-up'' process. Now transfer your weight to the left ski and rotate your body to the right side. Your left hand is now ahead and in front of your body. You have completed the ''unwind'' stage and your turn is completed. As you can see, turning is really just a matter of weight transfer and follow-through.

To complete a left-hand turn, wind-up to the right, transfer your weight to the right ski, and unwind to the left. Again, the best place to practise is on a gentle slope where the snow is reasonably well packed.

Once you feel comfortable with the snowplow turn and have learned the basic body movements and weight transfer techniques, it is relatively simple to progress to the more sophisticated turns. The turns you will now be learning are simply natural extensions of the snowplow turn. It is useful to know all the different types of turns because you will derive immense pleasure from being able to execute them correctly. Your skiing technique will be much more fluid, you will conserve energy, and the time taken to cover a measured course will be reduced dramatically.

''Stem Christie'' turn. As you gain confidence, you will want to try the Stem Christie turn. The basic snowplow turning principles still apply, with the only difference being that instead of assuming a full snowplow position, you assume a half-snowplow position. In other words, one ski continues almost straight ahead. The other ski is angled as in the full snowplow position. The weight transfer, wind-up, and unwind are then made and

the turn is completed. The movements for the Stem Christie are done more quickly than in the snowplow turn.

Let's run through a right-hand Stem Christie turn. As you are heading downhill and want to turn right, your left ski remains almost on a straight line. Your right ski is moved into the half-snowplow position. Now place your weight briefly on the right ski, forcing the inside edge into the snow. This move is called a "check" or "jam." At the same time, you windup to the left. Then you quickly unwind and transfer your weight to the left ski. Hold your position and follow through to the completion of the turn.

Stem Christie Turn

Parallel turn. The final step in turning, once you have mastered the Christie, is the parallel turn. It is really a sophisticated version of the Stem Christie and is accomplished without the use of a check or jam. The parallel turn is based purely on weight transfer and timing. The key to the parallel turn is the "lifting" of the weight off the skis and direct transfer of weight without using the wind-up-and-unwind method. The parallel turn requires perfect timing.

The lift is achieved by straightening up the legs from the normal downhill position. When your legs are straight, transfer your weight to complete the turn. The parallel turn on cross-country skis requires a great deal of experience and constant practice.

Standing step turn. If you want to turn left, lift the tip of the left ski off the ground and move the tip one foot to the left. The tail of the left ski is used as a pivot. Now lift the entire right ski

Parallel Turn

Standing Step Turn

Moving Step Turn

and bring it around to a position parallel to the left ski. The
process can then be repeated by lifting the tip of the left ski
another foot to the left, and so on.

In order to turn right, lift the tip of the right ski off the
ground, moving the tip one foot to the right. The left ski is then
lifted off the ground and brought around to a position parallel
to the right ski.

Moving step turn. The moving step turn is a handy turn to use
when skiing downhill, particularly around gentle turns. If done
correctly it also helps to maintain fluidity of movement and
momentum.

This turn is basically the same as the standing step turn. Once
you are moving downhill, take a small step with the right or left
ski (depending on which way you want to turn). We will run
through a right-hand step turn.

Move your right ski eight to twelve inches to the right. At the
exact moment that you lift your right ski for the first step, use
your left pole to push yourself to the right. The poling action

helps to maintain balance. Immediately after taking the step to the right, lift your left ski off the ground and bring it around so that it is parallel to the right ski. If balance is maintained at this stage, another step to the right can now be made. When executing a left turn, a step to the left is taken with push-off thrust coming from the right pole.

Practise the moving step turn on a gentle slope and keep the steps small until you acquire confidence. Also, keep your weight on the heels of the ski and maintain a crouch position at all times. Practise both left and right turns with the emphasis on your weak side.

Kick turn. The kick turn not only impresses the novice skiers around you but is a very practical turn that can be used for an abrupt change of direction. At the same time, it takes little space to complete and can be quickly executed with little effort.

Let's go through the mechanics of a right-hand kick turn. Stand on flat ground with the poles in normal position. Shift most of your weight to the left ski and move the left pole further to the left and slightly forward. Use the poles to maintain balance.

Kick Turn

Lean slightly forward on the left ski and lift the right ski straight forward and up so that the ski is at a 45° angle to the ground. The tail of the right ski is now resting on the ground at a point halfway between your left foot and the tip of the left ski.

Now, rotate your body 90° to the right and simultaneously move the right pole around to the right so that it is behind your body. It is now on the same side as the left pole.

At this point everything except your left foot and left ski has been swung around to the right. Swing your right ski around another 90° to the right and place it flat on the snow.

The left ski is still pointing in its original direction. The right ski is pointing in the opposite direction. (You won't want to stay in this position very long.)

Shift the weight now to the right ski, give a gentle push with both poles, and lift the left pole and left ski a few inches off the ground and swing it 180° to the right. Put the left ski on the snow so that it is parallel to the right ski. You have now completed the kick turn.

Practise both the right-hand and the left-hand kick turn on a regular basis, and it will soon become second nature to you. The kick turn can also be executed on a hill providing that you lean into the hill and dig your edges into the snow for stability.

Climbing Techniques

As mentioned earlier, the rapid weighting and unweighting method in exaggerated form is an ideal method of ascending moderately steep inclines (providing your wax is working properly).

Herringbone. The other most common method of climbing steep hills is called the "herringbone" method—so called because of the V-shape that is formed. Keeping the back straight and bending at the knees, spread the tips of the skis far apart with the tails together to form a large V. Lift one ski off the ground and plant it into the hill so that the inside edge digs into the snow. Now lift the trailing ski and plant it in the same way ahead of

Herringbone

Parallel Side Step

the other ski. It should be lifted far enough ahead of the other ski for the tail of the ski to clear the tail of the other ski. Continue to alternate each ski until you reach the top of the hill. The use of the poles remains the same as in the diagonal stride. Constant practice will help you increase your leg speed in lifting and planting alternating skis.

Parallel side step climbing. A slow but sure method of ascending a hill is the parallel side step method. Stand sideways to the hill with both skis parallel to one another. Lift the upper ski and plant it parallel approximately twelve inches above the lower ski (toward the top of the hill).

Make sure your weight is on the upper ski with the outside edge digging into the snow. Now bring the lower ski up to within six inches of the upper ski with the inside edge digging into the snow. Remember, the skis are always parallel to one another. You have now completed one step. Repeat the process by lifting the upper ski and once again planting it twelve inches ahead of the lower ski and so on.

As you become more confident and adept with this method the speed at which you ascend a hill will increase significantly. Keep practising and have patience.

Chapter Five
Telemarking

AFTER YOU HAVE MASTERED the basic turning techniques and feel comfortable with the parallel turn, you may want to try something new: Telemarking. Actually, Telemarking is just a new twist to one of the oldest known ski turns, which originated in the Telemark region of south-central Norway. It isn't really as difficult or mysterious as some people would have you believe. The Telemark is a swooping, knees-flexed turn developed as a better way to turn on skis with bindings that permit heel lift.

Find a gentle open slope that you can traverse at a slight angle. Most important, do some stretching exercises first to prevent pulled muscles and ligaments. Now take a few easy runs, practising the various turning techniques that you have learned so far. These few runs, including climbing, will loosen you up. Next practise the parallel turn. Remember to keep your skis close together as you glide down the hill. With your body facing down the hill, force your heels in the direction in which you want to turn. You should feel the inside (uphill) edges of your skis dig into the snow as your skis swing uphill.

Now let's visualize the Telemark turn. Even if you have never tried the maneuver, you have probably seen pictures of skiers doing it or have watched other skiers coming down hills making Telemark turns. Think of how their skis were scissored apart, their knees and ankles flexed, their upper bodies straight yet relaxed. Their hands should have been held low and out front, almost as if they were resting on the handlebars of a bicycle. Think about this position and you can imagine how it offers stability in all directions.

Now try out the position for yourself. Coast down the hill, skis parallel, body loose. When you come to any small bumps or dips in the terrain, relax and let your ankles and knees absorb the shock. Use your legs much like pistons. Don't fight the bumps, but rather ski right through them.

How are you holding your body? Is it still tense? Take a deep breath and try to relax all the way down the run. Remember to look down the slope ahead of you, not down at your ski tips. It's very important to develop confidence and agility on these straight runs before you tackle the actual Telemark turn.

How to Do the Telemark Turn

Let's rehearse the turn itself while standing still. Place your skis about shoulder width apart. Move your right foot backward about a step. Keep your left foot and the front of your right foot weighted, but let your right heel rise. With your back straight, flex your knees up and down. Your weight should be pressing

Telemark

down on the left (front) foot. Check if you are bending correctly after you have flexed your knees—you should not be able to see your front foot (in this case, the left foot). This is the Telemark position. Remember to stay basically over the center of your skis. If you lean too far forward you'll pitch over the tips of your skis; too much weight on your heels, and you'll fall backwards.

Now rock back and forth, feeling the difference between having your weight forward on your left foot and back on your right foot. It is essential to have your weight over your front ski to initiate a Telemark turn, so that it can carve into the snow.

Let's pretend that you want to turn right. With your weight on the left ski, rotate your left knee so that it turns into the hill (to the right) bending both knees as you twist. This is how you make your turns. Your left hip should follow through, pressing down the weight on the left ski as it becomes the driving force that causes the inside edge of your downhill ski (in this case, the left one) to dig into the snow.

In order to turn left, put your weight on the right, front ski. (Remember that the right ski is extended.) Rotate your right knee so that it turns into the hill (to the left). Use your right hip for the follow-through.

Although you might feel more comfortable with either your right or left front ski extended, it is important not to develop a favorite right- or left-turn habit. If you do, you will not get the full enjoyment out of Telemark skiing. Discipline yourself to practise turning equally to the right and to the left.

It's now time to try out all the theories on the slopes. First start to traverse the slope gradually. Then drop into the Telemark position. (Think ahead about which direction you want to turn.) Steer the turn up into the hill and gradually transfer weight to the rear ski until you stop. if you made a right turn, repeat the maneuver with a left turn. Next, try pointing your skis straight downhill and again carve out a single turn. Always alternate your turns to the right and to the left. At the completion of the turn, your upper body should be facing across the hill. Each turn is completed with equally weighted skis and signals the start of the next turn.

If you are having some difficulty, don't despair. Go back to basics. Try some snowplow or Stem Christie turns to reaquaint yourself with the feeling of steering and edging.

Pay attention to your poles as well. With your hands in the correct position, low and in front of you, your poles will angle behind you and out of the way. Incidentally many accomplished Telemark skiers use shorter, alpine-length poles to help keep their hands low and forward, since longer, Nordic-length poles tend to force you to stand up straighter, rather than low in the proper Telemark stance.

Once you've mastered single turns, the real enjoyment is just around the corner. The idea now is to link these looping turns into crisp, graceful arcs. Start off by steering yourself into a shallow or short Telemark turn. Now change lead skis as you rise up from your completed arc, and guide yourself into the next turn.

It is important to develop timing and rhythm in your turns. Try not to travel too far between turns. Keep the turns as tight as possible. It is most difficult to develop timing when the turns are too wide or drawn out.

Telemarking Equipment

You have probably noticed that I have not mentioned specific equipment for Telemark skiing. This omission was by design, as Telemarking can be done with light touring or even racing skis.

If, however, you go to an area where there are specific Telemarking hills or even downhill ski areas, it is wise and in some cases compulsory to have regular Telemarking equipment. My advice, once again, is to seek out a shop that has knowledgeable staff who have actually participated in Telemark skiing.

Skis. On the advice of just such a store in the Toronto area—Muskoka Windsurfing—I tried two lines of skis and arrived at the following conclusions, which I have put in chart form. Before we take a look at my findings, I should point out that I noticed a great difference between my cross-country racing skis and those designed for Telemarking. Telemarking skis provide extra stability because of their wider width. Telemarking skis also have metal edges that allow you to carve out a turn with far greater ease and control.

As a former downhill racer, I got back that old feeling of power and speed as I Telemarked my way down a steep descent. I must admit that I loved every minute of my experience, but not enough to give up cross-country skiing and concentrate solely on Telemarking. Possibly next season I'll invest in a pair of Telemark skis and enjoy the best of both worlds—cross-country and Telemarking.

Boots. Karhu's Challenger and Endurance boots are both ideal for Telemark skiing. The Challenger is a medium-cut boot while the Endurance features a double boot for added support and warmth.

The Alpine boot is a double leather boot with reinforced pin-holes at the toe. It is also an excellent hiking boot.

Bindings. I was most satisfied with Rottefella Telemark, Super Rottefella Telemark, and Villam bindings.

Poles. If you are specializing in Telemark skiing, invest in a pair of downhill poles for improved turn execution.

TELEMARKING EQUIPMENT

Name	Features	Comment
Karhu GT	Double camber ski with wax pocket; metal edges with P-Tex base	Excellent for off-track skiing; performance is fair on packed snow
Karhu Comp	Single camber ski; does not have a wax pocket; metal edges with P-Tex base	Excellent ski for beginner to advanced Telemark skier; has good edging ability; strong and durable
Kozama Mountain Soft	Single camber ski; has soft flex; offset edges with P-Tex base	Good performance in powder; excellent turning ski; recommended for advanced to expert skiers
Kozama Mountain High	Double camber ski; P-Tex base	Versatile ski; good for off-track and Telemarking; has a tendency to wash out during turns
Kozama Telemark	Single camber ski with firm flex; P-Tex base	Excellent performance ski under icy conditions; recommended for experts and racers

Chapter Six
Non-Competitive Touring

ONCE YOU HAVE COMPLETED distances of up to fifteen kilometers
with relative ease, you may wish to test your skills by entering
a recognized tour. Your first tour should not be too long. I recommend a distance of approximately fifteen kilometers.

Touring Tips

Wax for grip, not slip. For middle and long distances remember
this advice. You will be thankful you did, especially during those
long uphill climbs. Always carry one wax that is softer than the
wax of the day with you as well. Remember, temperatures can
change as the day progresses.

Set a goal. Your objective should be to finish the tour strongly,
without undo strain. If you want to set a time objective for yourself, fine, but be realistic. Only you know the pace at which you
feel comfortable.

Pace yourself. The key to achieving your goals in middle- and
long-distance events is a combination of patience and pacing.
Over the years I have watched a great many skiers who sprinted
from the starting line only to drop out later from exhaustion. I
have also seen several sad cases of hypothermia which accom-
panies exhaustion. Remember, it is better to start slowly and finish strongly than to start too quickly and not finish at all. Don't
start at the front of the pack. Pick a midpoint.

Pair up with another skier. Ski with someone who is setting the same pace as yourself. As the kilometers pass, you can either increase or decrease your speed. Always let someone else be the "pacer" whenever possible. If you are gasping for breath, you are going too fast. Slow down and relax.

Stop at all feeding stations. Take advantage of every opportunity to replenish your body with energy food. Drink a full cup of water or glucose mixture whenever it is offered or you will risk dehydration. If there are no feeding stations, carry liquid refreshments with you to replenish your body's water loss.

During my first tour I made the critical error of skipping a feeding station under the false impression that I would make up valuable time. I laughed as I passed fifty or more skiers who had stopped to take on nourishment. They had the last laugh as all but one or two of the skiers waved goodbye to me near the end of the tour.

Maintain a rhythm. Once you establish rhythm, maintain it as long as you are able. There is no better feeling than that of having all parts of your body working in sync with one another. You will be saving valuable energy as well.

Combat fatigue. As fatigue begins to set in, you may want to give your legs a rest for awhile by double poling only. Similarly, you might rest your arms for a short period of time by dropping them to your sides and using the kick-and-glide action without poles.

Concentrate on your weaknesses. A long-distance event presents a perfect situation to practise your double pole, single kick routine. Practise kicking with first one leg and then the other. You could also concentrate on your skating technique when the trail permits. Think positive thoughts and you will succeed. After you experience the elation of crossing the finishing line, don't forget to stretch your muscles and keep warm. A short walk is also an excellent method of cooling down.

Then, finally, you can reward yourself with a hot toddy and enjoy the camaraderie of your fellow skiers. They will no doubt have interesting tales to tell. Most important, you will always remember that moment when you crossed the finish line, having just completed a distance that you had previously thought impossible.

Family Touring

The sport of cross-country skiing is an ideal family pursuit. Although each family member has his or her own hobbies and personal interests, it is usually possible to set aside one day of the week when the entire family can head for the trails.

Once you have bought your equipment, it is a very economical sport to pursue. Many ski areas now offer season memberships at very reasonable rates. If you pay as you ski, the current rates per day range from $4.00 for adults to as little as $1.50–$2.00 for children or juniors. Compare these rates to those charged by the downhill resorts and you can see the excellent value offered by cross-country.

Getting the Family Started

Once the non-skiing members of the family have decided to give it a try, a decision must be made regarding equipment. Before investing your hard-earned dollars in equipment I suggest that you rent boots, poles, and skis for the first few outings. At the end of this period, it should be obvious whether or not the novice likes the sport enough to warrant an investment in the necessary gear. An alternative to the buying or renting of equipment is the use of "hand-me-down" poles, boots, and skis. Be very careful, however, to make sure that the poles are the correct length, that the skis are the correct camber, and that the boots fit properly.

The Correct Approach with Beginners

If there is one avid skier in the family, it is up to that person to give guidance and lend assistance. That first outing can turn youngsters into avid, lifetime ski buffs or it can make them feel that they never again want to put on a pair of skis. Incidentally, when I say "first outing," I am referring to the first visit to a resort with machine-groomed tracks. Beginners should have previously tried out their skis locally at a park or golf course.

Experienced skiers, even if they are the competitive type, must exhibit the patience of Job. It is not an easy task. By giving you a personal glimpse at how I helped my son develop his skiing abilities, I hope to help you understand how best to handle the situation. I am not suggesting that my method is the only one that works; I am only proffering it as an example.

I treated Kevin as an equal the first time out. I took off on the trail normally, with him in pursuit. After a few minutes, he yelled at me to slow down as he was falling further and further behind. Frustrated, I turned around, retraced my tracks and reached his side. It was then that I saw the light. I had to teach him the intricacies of the sport or I would lose him as a skiing buddy forever.

Bit by bit, step by step, I gave him the basics in techniques, and he absorbed it all. As he was afraid of becoming lost, I assured him that I would ski ahead of him, but that I would return periodically to check his progress and to reassure him.

Occasionally he would yell at me to slow down and wait for him. Although it may sound cruel, I never slowed my pace. I simply told him that he had to ski faster, and he did. I always kept a watchful eye on him, however, and knew exactly where he was at all times. I constantly returned to his side to check his progress and to encourage him about his style or progress. He was determined to improve even more, as a result of my encouragement.

I soon learned that I was helping myself as well as my son. I even started to take my own advice to improve my own technique. Also, by repeatedly retracing my tracks, I was increasing my own workload and developing much-needed stamina. Kevin and I were, all of a sudden, a compatible twosome—team members making progress together.

As Kevin became stronger and his speed increased, I devised games to make him go even faster. For example, I would buy him a drink or chocolate bar if he could finish one lap of a 2.5-kilometer course before I could finish two. Kevin began to look forward to these little competitions and so did I. We were both improving by leaps and bounds.

As he grew and became stronger over the years, I had to reduce my handicap. The competitions became keener and keener as he edged closer to his old dad. We truly loved the competition, and we loved each other's company. We talked endlessly during our drive to and from the ski trails about technique, waxing, and strategy. When I sensed that he was tiring of ski talk, I dropped the subject until he brought it up again.

One day, after a good workout, Kevin asked me if I could enter him in a ten-kilometer race. He felt that he was ready; I knew he was ready.

Kevin won that race and after receiving his gold medal decided that he was going to enter a marathon event: the prestigious Kawartha Ski Tour and Race. The distance involved for his age category was a fifty-kilometer event scheduled over two days. I laid out a training schedule to which we religiously adhered over a four-week period. We were both ready when the big day arrived.

As has always been my policy, I discussed strategy, particularly the importance of pacing, with Kevin just before the first day's competition. Kevin's event and my own overlapped for the first day. We both had to ski twenty-five kilometers the first day. Kevin had to ski twenty-five kilometers the second day as well. I had to ski fifty kilometers on the second day.

Ignoring my strategy to start slowly, Kevin burst out of the starting gate in grand fashion. He was going to annihilate his fellow competitors and walk away with the competition. He was going to show up his old dad. He almost succeeded in his goal.

A scant three kilometers from the finish line, Kevin started to feel the effects of dehydration and was on the verge of developing hypothermia—a dangerous reduction of body temperature. His pace slowed to a standstill, and other skiers passed him with ease. He managed to finish on rubber legs. He had learned a valuable lesson; pacing oneself is critical.

Kevin did not make the same mistake the following year at Kawartha. Pacing himself almost perfectly, he won the silver medal for boys from seventeen to eighteen years over the seventy-five-kilometer distance. The year after that Kevin finally achieved his ultimate goal. He won the gold medal for his age category.

Family Ski Vacations
Many people who used to hate winter with its snow and bitter cold start to enjoy the season after being introduced to cross-country skiing. They discover, by dressing correctly and by becoming proficient at this sport, that their old hatred of the cold was unjustified.

The Florida vacation becomes a thing of the past. These new

devotees now want to take a vacation in the "great white north." The choices available are many and varied. You can stay at a lodge, go hut-to-hut, yurt-to-yurt, or lodge to lodge.

Our family spent a week in northern Ontario at a resort called Pinestone Inn in Haliburton, and we had a super vacation. My son and I were out skiing the freshly groomed tracks at the crack of dawn each day and then joined my wife and daughter after breakfast for a full day's skiing. We were completely spoiled at this resort, which had all the amenities: pool, whirlpool, sauna, games room, excellent cuisine, and a lively nightlife. We returned home more relaxed and refreshed after that vacation than after any one we had taken previously (or, for that matter, since).

For the more adventurous and hardy skiers who are not "softies" like us, I would recommend a hut-to-hut tour. The organizers provide a guide, food, and the opportunity to tour the great outdoors at a reasonable pace. You certainly won't have any of the amenities at your fingertips, but you will learn how to live in harmony with nature, and come away with a new respect for it.

I would not recommend hut-to-hut touring for adults or teenagers who do not like camping or who do not like the challenge of the more rugged back-country touring. These camps, in other words, are for the hard-core, dedicated skier.

Each day's skiing ends at a different cabin which contains bunks and a woodstove. Hot meals are served and a comfortable night's sleep is your reward. Some people prefer hut-to-hut touring to regular touring because it has a sense of destination, in contrast to a resort where the trail ends up where it began. You wake up each morning in new surroundings and in anticipation of a completely new adventure.

Yurt-to-yurt touring is similar to hut-to-hut with the only difference being the form of the shelter. A yurt is a luxury tent approximately ten feet tall perched on a solid log platform. It is circular in shape and is supported by floor-to-ceiling stakes and wooden latticework that reaches up its sides. It is topped by a skylight to allow for stargazing at night.

I should point out that in both hut-to-hut and yurt-to-yurt touring, the comfort level is dictated by the style and quality of your outfitter.

There is no doubt, however, that anyone who associates ski camping with cold, pain, and misery will think differently once he trys it. Believe it or not, some outfitters even serve four-course gourmet dinners accompanied by hot spiced wine.

Lodge-to-lodge touring is a more sophisticated version of the hut-to-hut and yurt-to-yurt concepts. A number of lodges cooperate in a "ski-through" program whereby you stay at a different lodge each night. All the lodges involved are located and joined together along a specific trail system.

The advantage of the lodge-to-lodge concept, aside from the obvious amenities it affords you, is that you can arrange to have your luggage and even your car shuttled from lodge to lodge. With service like this, you are relieved of the necessity of carrying heavy packs on the trail during the day.

The Haliburton Highlands Nordic Trail Association, in cooperation with the government of Ontario, Carling-O'Keefe Breweries, and a number of townships in the Haliburton area, is now developing a linked-trail system of approximately 320 kilometers. This trail system will be available to the general public and the competitive skier.

The 320 kilometers of recreational trails will link together seven major cross-country lodges in the Haliburton region—Haliburton Lodge, Pinestone Inn, Maple Sands Resort, Locarno Resort, Sandy Lane, Sir Sams Inn, and Silver Eagle Resort—for an inn-to-inn touring network that will match the best in Quebec and New England.

A recently completed World Cup course of fifty kilometers is now located close to the town of Haliburton and the Pinestone Inn and Country Club. An official bid for the 1989 fifty-kilometer World Cup is soon to be made to the appropriate authorities. It is envisioned that Haliburton will become the Nordic capital of the southern part of Ontario, in both competitive and recreational arenas.

Chapter Seven

Seniors: The New Breed of Cross-Country Skiers

IN CANADA WE HAVE the Jackrabbit program for young skiers (twelve years of age and under), racing programs for teenagers, and citizens' races for the middle-aged "crazies" like myself. Almost unnoticed is a new breed of cross-country skiers—retirees—who are invading cross-country resorts in record numbers across Canada and the United States. Surprisingly, according to many instructors, almost half of their students are retirees. Why the sudden boom?

Many seniors take up skiing simply as a way to eliminate "cabin fever" when it's snowing, others for the satisfaction of learning something new. Many start up to enjoy the beauty of the woods during the winter months. One thing that they all have in common is a love of the great outdoors and a strong desire to stay healthy and fit.

For aerobics, muscle toning, and weight control, cross-country skiing ranks as the number-one exercise. A lot of people have complemented the activities they do during the summer months—like golf, biking, and hiking—with cross-country skiing so that they can stay in shape all year long. One of the advantages of Nordic skiing is that everyone can ski at his or her own pace. Participation can vary from a leisurely afternoon ski tour to a twenty-kilometer race. The pace can be as strenuous or relaxing as you want it to be.

An obvious advantage to the sport is that cross-country skiing introduces you to new friends from all walks of life. Many people find that after retiring they have too much idle time on their hands.

A lot of people get started by checking with their local parks and recreation departments, ski shops, or cross-country resorts. Many facilities offer organized classes or tours. After they learn the basics of cross-country, they often organize a group of new friends from the class and ski together once or twice a week.

If you join a group, it's much more likely that you will go out on a regular basis. When you ski by yourself, it's too easy to postpone a tour if the weather is less than promising or if you have another pressing commitment. Group skiing is also much safer. If you get hurt, someone can go for help. It is best to ski with two or three other skiers. Also, it is only common sense not to leave a slower skier behind on the trail. The fastest and most skilled skier can always ski back and forth on a double tracked trail to check the slower skier's progress. By so doing, the faster skier can get in an even more beneficial workout!

The initial experience for all cross-country skiers sets the tone for their attitude towards the sport. If their first experience is rewarding, chances are they will want to pursue cross-country skiing with vigor and determination for years to come. The outcome of that first experience usually depends on good equipment. I recommend waxless skis for the older first-time skiers. It may be wise to rent cross-country gear for the first couple of times until you find out whether or not the sport is for you. If you enjoy the sport, talk to other skiers you know as well as to reliable ski shops before you buy all the necessary equipment. Some ski shops apply first-time rental fees to the purchase price if you decide to buy.

Once you have made the commitment to take up the sport, I would strongly urge you to seek out a qualified instructor. Sign up for five or six lessons. I'm certain that you will agree later that the lessons were an excellent investment. Although you can learn from well-meaning friends, you risk picking up bad skiing habits that might be difficult to correct later on.

For retirees, the opportunities to become relatively skilled at

Nordic skiing are greater than for the average working person who is limited to weekend skiing. Theirs to enjoy during the work week are the uncrowded trails, virtually deserted save for the odd group of schoolchildren on a day trip, who tend to spend the greater part of the day at special instructional areas off the main trails. Talk to the resort owner and arrange for a group or individual lesson during this slow period. Almost certainly you will get far more out of a lesson when the instructor is not pressed for time. You will be better able to relax as well. Enjoy the sport and the surrounding beauty of nature.

If you are the competitive type, that's fine; but be realistic in the goals you set for yourself. First of all, ski a distance that is comfortable for you, and build from that point. If, for example, you are able to ski a fifteen-kilometer trail with ease and want to increase the distance to twenty-five kilometers after four or five weeks of training, don't ski a trail that is marked twenty-five kilometers in length. Be smart; and add two to five kilometer loops that are in close proximity to the chalet. If you encounter unforeseen difficulties, you will be able to rest and recover in warmth and comfort. If you were able to ski twenty-five kilometers without straining this way, then and only then should you challenge the twenty-five-kilometer trail.

My advice, if you are bent on entering citizens' races or time trials in the future, is to ignore the competitive aspect for the first season. Enter a non-competitive mass participation ski tour. Select a distance that you feel is within your capability. By skiing this distance at your regular pace, or perhaps slightly above it, you will learn more about your physical strengths and weaknesses than you ever thought possible. At the conclusion of this tour, you and only you will be able to assess your progress and plan future endeavors intelligently. If you always remember to train, not strain, you will be amazed at the remarkable progress that can be made in a relatively short period of time.

Part Three
The Competitive Edge

Competitive Touring and Citizens' Races • Marathon Skiing • Racing

If you want to be competitive, you must be prepared to work hard. The most expensive pair of skis and boots teamed up with the best-looking racing suit do not guarantee that you will be a winner. It takes dedicated training and a burning desire to achieve perfection if you are to reach your goals. I am addressing the average skier who wants to rise above the crowd and ultimately find a place on the podium. I achieved my personal goals by using a trial-and-error method, and now I am passing on my methods to others in the hope that their dreams will come true.

If you follow my methods and race strategies and are willing to get out of bed on a sub-zero morning for a workout, you can't help but achieve your own goals. Be consistent, be dedicated, follow a training regimen every day, and you will do it. I guarantee it will work. Good luck!

Chapter Eight
Competitive Touring and Citizens' Races

YOU HAVE COMPLETED your first tour and season and your appetite has been whetted for the more competitive side of cross-country skiing. Before we take a look at the various types of events that are scheduled, let's consider the approach that you should take in preparing for such events.

Preparation and Planning for Marathons

Review your equipment. It is to your advantage to invest in a good pair of racing skis if you haven't already done so. Racing skis are lighter, narrower, and faster than regular touring skis. I have a pair of fifty-millimeter skis that are very satisfactory for any event that I care to enter. Also, I would suggest that you invest in racing bindings and boots.

In my opinion it is not a good idea to have the wider bindings from your touring skis mounted on racing skis. I discovered the hard way that the wider bindings tend to brush against the sides of machine-groomed tracks, causing friction and thereby retarding the gliding capability.

Most skiers have neither the time nor the funds to enter more than a few major weekend events during the season, particularly those involving out-of-town travel and accommodation. I recommend that you determine the event or events you want to enter as early in the season as possible.

Commit yourself. Make a personal commitment by mailing in your entry at the earliest possible date. By so doing you will force yourself into a training schedule early in order to ensure that you will complete your goal.

Follow a training program of approximately eight to ten weeks duration. In addition to the exercise program that I outlined in Chapter Three, it is absolutely essential that you cover as many kilometers as possible on the trails. Since most skiers do not live in close proximity to groomed trails where they are able to train before or after school or work, they must settle for workouts at the local golf course or park during the work or school week. The weekend training can be done on groomed trails.

Remember, the muscles used in cross-country skiing are different from those used in any other sport. The ski movement and coordination of muscle groups cannot be simulated by any other exercise, although roller skiing is a close second to the real thing. If you have been training on roller skis, continue to do so as long as weather permits. The key to a successful season is still actual on-snow practice and repetition.

Begin slowly. If the ski season is just beginning, don't overdo it for the first few outings. The old adage ''train, don't strain'' still holds true. Ski until you are tired but not exhausted, even if you have only skied five kilometers. Don't worry about speed at the start of the season. Concentrate, rather, on style and on what you learned during the last winter. Do some stretching exercises after your workout as well as before and call it a day. Regardless of how hard you trained in the off-season, some stiffness and soreness will occur, particularly in the groin area. Repeat the same distance during the next six workouts.

Build endurance. When you feel comfortable at around the five-kilometer distance, try skiing ten kilometers nonstop. Take a break and ski another ten kilometers nonstop. Take a break and ski another ten kilometers. Repeat this distance for the next five or six workouts. Now you should be ready to ski back-to-back ten-kilometer runs or twenty kilometers nonstop (depending on your overall conditioning, of course).

I find that it is wise to save the long workouts for weekends when it is possible to ski on machine-groomed trails. Incidentally, when training over a ten-kilometer loop, I always leave a drink of water in the snow and take on some liquid before starting the second ten-kilometer loop. Always have water at your disposal in order to avoid dehydration.

Use the "Moment of Truth" test. Once you have skied a twenty-kilometer run nonstop during six different workouts, the next step, which I call the "Moment of Truth" test, is to ski twenty kilometers in the morning and twenty kilometers in the afternoon, one day per week. Repeat over the course of three or four weekends.

A heavy workout like this should be followed by a light workout if you are skiing the next day. Reduce your distance by 50 percent or to twenty kilometers to allow your body to recover. Once you are able to ski up to sixty kilometers on a weekend, you can complete a fifty-kilometer "time trial," or competitive tour, in reasonably good time.

Do speed and hill training workouts. Once you have achieved the sixty-kilometer weekend workload, take the next day off and rest. Do some light calisthenics to maintain flexibility. Set aside at least one day a week for speed and hill training workouts if possible. Select an uphill slope approximately one kilometer in length. Ski up the hill as quickly as possible from bottom to top. Glide back down to the start and repeat five or six times. After repeating the exercise over six outings, you may want to increase the repetitions to ten or twelve times nonstop. These workouts will strengthen the quadriceps and improve cardiovascular endurance. The downhill portion will improve form by improving kick and relaxation.

Leave time for a taper-off period. During the last week before your event, reduce your mileage significantly. I recommend that you ski a total distance of fifteen kilometers over three easy workouts. Continue to do your normal stretching and conditioning exercises, and go for a brisk five-kilometer walk the day before your event in order to stay loose.

Watch your diet. Several days before any long-distance event, start to "load up" on carbohydrates in order to store up that much needed energy. Foods rich in carbohydrates are converted to glycogen and stored in the muscles. Reduce the amount of meat you eat, especially hamburgers and hot dogs. Drastically reduce your sugar intake, and avoid bacon, French-fried potatoes, cream, and ice cream.

Pre-Race Preparation
- Study a map of the race course carefully. Know exactly where you will be skiing before you start.
- Check snow conditions and temperature and wax early.
- Warm up properly through stretching exercises.
- Ski a slow one or two kilometers. Rewax if your present wax is not right.
- Check all equipment carefully to make sure it is in good working order.

The Marathon Race: Strategies

- Don't start too fast. Let the eager beavers battle it out. Chances are they will fade early.
- Think technique at all times. Avoid "scrambling" on your skis. Each slip and misplaced pole placement will cost you dearly both in time and lost energy.
- Establish a rhythm early and concentrate on maintaining it.
- Racing, in addition to being physically punishing, is psychologically demanding as well. As the race progresses, it is far easier on a skier's mental outlook to be able to pass another skier than to be passed. I find it beneficial, therefore, to focus on one skier at a time and to pass that skier when the opportunity presents itself.
- As the race wears on, use the downhill sections to rest your arms and to breathe deeply and slowly.
- Always stop at every feeding station to take on liquid refreshment. Use these stops to ease aching muscles by doing flexibility exercises such as touching your toes or squatting.
- Stay mentally alert. Chastise yourself for becoming careless. Play games with yourself; imagine that you are floating on a cushion of air, that you are skiing for an Olympic gold medal. These thoughts may sound zany, but they work.
- Above all else, you must be determined to ski "through the pain." Think positive thoughts and you will do it. Once you approach that finish line and hear the crowd clapping and cheering in recognition of your achievement, you will indeed feel like an Olympic champion!

Events in Canada

There are numerous tours, races, and other incentive programs across Canada. Here is an east-to-west rundown of just a few of the highlights with which I am familiar. In all cases, for further details on these and the many other events being held each season, contact local ski clubs, or check current issues of *North Country Skier: Canada's Cross-Country Ski Journal*. (Subscribe to: North Country Skier, 45 Woodhurst Drive, Sault Ste. Marie, Ontario P6C 5Z5.)

Generally speaking, when you see or hear the word "tour," chances are that the elite competitive skiers will not be entered. There are, however, exceptions to the rule. In some events there are both elite and citizens' classes. ("Citizen," in this context, refers to the recreational competitor.) Some events require a competitor's card which is easily obtained through the specific provincial zone office involved.

Newfoundland and Labrador
There are a variety of cross-country skiing events held every year in Newfoundland and Labrador. Memorial University of Newfoundland hosts a meet in St. John's in January. The Provincial Cross-Country Skiing Championships and the Syenite Invitational Cross-Country Ski Meet are held in February. In March, the Newfoundland Cross-Country Ski Marathon is held in Gander and a family cross-country skiing loppet is held in the Happy Valley/Goose Bay area of Labrador. The loppet is organized by the Birchbrook Nordic Ski Club, which also offers four-day overnight tours. For more information, consult the annual book of events and attractions published by the Department of Development and Tourism.

New Brunswick
New Brunswick is becoming increasingly important for its cross-country skiing events. Ski marathons are held at Kouchibouguac National Park every year. There is also an event known as the Fraser Cup Races and another called the Mountaineer's Cup,

both of which take place at Sugarloaf Provincial Park. Information about these events can be obtained from any of the cross-country ski clubs in the province.

Nova Scotia

Nova Scotia's list of cross-country events is growing each year in direct proportion to the ever-increasing popularity of the sport. One of the most popular events of the skiing season in Nova Scotia is the Island Games, held annually in Cape North. Numerous cross-country categories for all ages over varying distances make this event a memorable experience.

Quebec

The province of Quebec is truly a cross-country skier's paradise as far as the number and choice of events is concerned. One of the most popular events or series of events is the Quebec Loppet Series, which offers thousands of skiers, from the novice competitor to the more seasoned veteran, the opportunity to participate. The series is open to everyone and allows skiers to compete against other skiers in the same age group and at the same level of ability. You can choose short-, middle-, or long-distances in every competition.

Another event, the Smith-Johannsen Loppet, is of special interest to me because it was founded in 1972 in honor of Herman Smith-Johannsen. The awards are also special. Time standard pins are awarded to those finishing within a certain time limit. In addition, certificates with a photo of "Jackrabbit" Johannsen are awarded to all finishers.

The highlight of the cross-country ski season in Quebec (and many would say in Canada) is the Canadian Ski Marathon. The world-famous Canadian Ski Marathon is the longest two-day cross-country tour in the world and is annually attended by several thousand cross-country skiers from at least a dozen countries. The Canadian Ski Marathon is not a race but a tour ideally suited to all skiers of all ages and abilities. How far you ski is up to you, from sixteen kilometers to the full 160 kilometers. Participants can enter and qualify for awards as individuals and/or as teams.

The CSM begins at Lachute and follows 160 kilometers of double-tracked trail through the picturesque landscape of western Quebec to the finish on the famous Rideau Canal in the heart of Ottawa. The route is composed of ten sections, five open for use on Saturday and the remainder on Sunday. Organized and run by experienced volunteers; the two-day event is an opportunity to spend an unusual ski-touring weekend without anxiety or risk. At the end of all ten sections, hot drinks and snacks are served and first-aid services and equipment repairs provided.

Ontario

The province of Ontario with its vast network of cross-country ski clubs and resorts offers unlimited opportunities for the competitive skier. Some competitive tours, such as the Kawartha Ski Tour and Race held at Apsley, Ontario, offer special incentives for every skier. The choice of distances ranges from ten kilometers to the demanding seventy-five-kilometer test. At the Kawartha Tour, medals are available to all skiers in different age categories who meet a certain time standard. You can achieve a bronze medal one year and progress through the silver and gold stages to the ''Award of Excellence.'' In this category you are really competing against the clock. There are also other awards to aim for, such as medals for the top three finishers in each age category. The northern part of the province affords you the opportunity to enjoy nature's finest wilderness surroundings. Another event I highly recommend is the Algonquin Marathon, a two-day event held in the heart of the Algonquin Park wilderness. The groomed tracks are truly world class, the surroundings exquisite, and the people friendly and hospitable. You can choose either a twenty-five-kilometer or a fifty-kilometer event depending on whether you are a novice skier or an expert racer.

Traveling farther north to the Thunder Bay area, you may wish to participate in the Sibley Ski Tour. The tour takes place at Sibley Provincial Park, situated about fifty kilometers from Thunder Bay. Participating skiers can test their skills and endurance over a twenty-, forty-, or fifty-kilometer, double tracked distance. The elite skiers treat this tour as a top-level marathon race; but most skiers simply enjoy the unsurpassed beauty of the surroundings, the socializing, and a day of unforgettable skiing.

Manitoba

Manitoba has a unique events program for the avid cross-country skier. There are two different series in which to participate.

The first series, the Manitoba Loppet Series, consists of eight races per year, each race taking place at a different site. The age groups vary from seven and under to the thirty-five to thirty-nine (masters) age group. Individual awards are presented at the conclusion of the series.

The second series, the Swix Participation Races, are held weekly depending on snow conditions at one site—Windsor Park Golf Course. The unusual aspect to this series is the lack of emphasis on age-group categories. Skiers, regardless of age, are classified as to their ability after the first race and are seeded up or down as the season progresses. Annual age-class awards, however, are retained.

Saskatchewan

The Saskatchewan 60 Cross-Country Marathon, only one of the numerous events scheduled, is a fixture on the cross-country scene in Saskatchewan and is fast becoming a national event. The event is held each year in Nisbet Forest near Duck Lake. Entries in this well-organized event are limited to the first 900 entrants, so plan your schedule well in advance.

The Saskatchewan Ski Association also coordinates the scheduling of a series of loppets throughout the province in conjunction with local clubs that act as hosts. In order to enter the loppet series you must first obtain a loppet passport from the Saskatchewan Ski Association office. The passport records each skier's participation, and medals and certificates are awarded as earned.

Alberta

The province of Alberta has a full schedule of cross-country loppets, marathons, and races for all skiers from the novice to the expert.

One event that has attracted considerable attention is the Sun Life Canadian Birkebeiner, which takes place near Devon, Alberta. The fifty-five-kilometer course is described as being both challenging and scenic with a number of climbs and descents in and out of the North Saskatchewan River valley. The finish line is most memorable as it is located on the main street of 1885 Fort

Edmonton, surrounded by the reconstructed buildings of nine-teenth-century Edmonton.

British Columbia

The province of British Columbia in the past few years has seen a tremendous surge in the number of cross-country ski events held throughout the province.

In an effort to promote participation in cross-country skiing, the Swix Company sponsored and continues to sponsor the British Columbia Loppet Series. The main purpose, other than participation, is to reward those who ski in cross-country ski marathons. If you ski three of the twelve marathons in the first season, your reward is a bronze pin. You are then eligible to go for silver and gold pins in succeeding years. There are now additional incentive awards, however.

I would be remiss if I did not mention the famous Cariboo Marathon, which takes place at the village of 100 Mile House, 300 miles north of Vancouver. The marathon, which covers a distance of fifty kilometers, starts at 108 Mile House and ends at downtown 100 Mile. The scenery is outstanding, the hospitality endearing, and the organizational excellence memorable. All the superlatives used to describe the Cariboo Marathon must be true when over 1,600 skiers register each year! Register early and go for the "I Did It" pin that is awarded when you cross that finish line.

Incentive Award Programs in Canada

The Jackrabbit Ski League

It is generally agreed that young children should not be pushed into the competition aspect of cross-country skiing. It is most important that children enjoy the sport and form a love for nature and the great outdoors while they participate at their own skill levels. The program has been kept low-key by design in the hope that young skiers will choose cross-country skiing as a lifelong pursuit.

The Jackrabbit Ski League, adopted nationally in 1980, is a program for children from eight to thirteen organized through the clubs and divisions of the Canadian Ski Association. It is designed to acquaint children not only with cross-country skiing, but also with the general concepts of fitness and nutrition.

The Jackrabbit Ski League provides a skill awards program to allow children to measure their progress and to experience the satisfaction of earning awards for their newly acquired skills. The league also offers a speed awards program.

Awards aside, participation is the key objective of any Jackrabbit program. Children are encouraged to participate at their own level of interest and expertise. The essential ingredient of all Jackrabbit activities is fun. Children can join the Jackrabbit Ski League through their local ski club, or they can form a club at their school or recreational centre.

For further information on Jackrabbits, contact:

Cross Country Canada
333 River Road
Ottawa, Ontario
K1L 8H9
(613) 741-1206

Other Incentive Awards for the Tourer

Many skiers, especially at the outset, do not want or need the competitive aspect of cross-country skiing. They would, however, like some recognition of their achievements over the course of the season. If this appeals to you, there are several alternatives to competitive skiing.

The Touring Distance awards program sponsored by the Canadian Ski Association is a national program. These awards are available to any skier affiliated with a CSA club. The distance skied for an award must be completed for a single season. All loppets and other official-event distances may be added. The distances, location, and date skied are to be recorded on control cards that can be obtained through each division office. There is no charge for distance control cards. The completed distances are accepted on an honor system. The current touring distances are shown on the table on the next page.

The skiing community should take off their hats to the Carlsberg people for their commitment to the sport across the country. Their programs vary from province to province. In Ontario, Carlsberg's "Count The Kilometers" program has exceeded even the company's own expectations. If you are a skier in Ontario

TOURING DISTANCES

Category	Bronze	Silver	Gold
Men 17 and over	200 km	350 km	500 km
Women 17 and over	150 km	275 km	400 km
14-16 year olds	100 km	200 km	400 km
10-13 year olds	60 km	150 km	250 km
7-9 year olds	40 km	100 km	150 km

Note: The skier's age is his or her age at the time the required distance is completed.

and want some recognition for all those kilometers that you have been logging every weekend then this program is for you. Medals are awarded for skiing fifteen kilometers and twenty-five kilometers in one day.

For the skier who achieves 500 kilometers over one season, there is the Carlsberg 500-kilometer Plus Elite Division award. As a special incentive, the Carlsberg people offer a trophy to any skier who achieves the seemingly insurmountable task of skiing 1000 kilometers in one season. I can assure you that this feat is not impossible as even this old jackrabbit qualified for this trophy in the 1984/85 season.

Chapter Nine

Marathon Skiing: A Personal Glimpse

THE GATINEAU 55 is Canada's only Worldloppet race and is open to cross-country skiers seventeen years of age and over. The event attracts about 1500 skiers from around the world and represents one of the greatest challenges that any skier will ever encounter. It is considered the most prestigious loppet in Canada.

The Gatineau Park lies within 466,000-hectare national capital region and just within the western border of Quebec about eighteen kilometers northwest of Ottawa. To the south it extends like an elongated thumb into the ever-expanding city of Hull, Quebec; to the north the park fades into the never-never land of the shield country of the Eardley plateau and Gatineau hills. To the west, the park plunges some 250 meters to the Ottawa River over the Eardley escarpment. The terrain is sparsely populated with hardwoods and evergreens and exemplifies winter wilderness.

This event is organized by the Canadian Ski Marathon Incorporated, a non-profit organization, in cooperation with the National Capital Commission. By entering the race, a skier becomes a voting member of CSM for the current year.

(Incidentally, there is also a thirty-five-kilometer touring event for the non-competitive skiers. The minimum age limit for this event is twelve years. There are no class awards or medals of achievement given for this event.)

The Worldloppet League is a circuit of ten cross-crountry ski races, each held in one of ten member countries throughout Europe and North America. Often referred to as the ''Citizens' Olympics'' in cross-country skiing, Worldloppet events are the challenge of a lifetime for any skier.

There are two distinct categories in the Worldloppet League: the Citizen class and the Elite class. The foremost purpose of the organization is to honor dedicated long-distance cross-country skiers who complete the courses in all of the official Worldloppet races. A passport will be issued to all cross-country skiers who want to attempt it. If they succeed, the Worldloppet League will issue them a diploma certifying their accomplishments. Receipt of this diploma in turn enables them to qualify for the prestigious Worldloppet gold medallion.

As further incentive to all skiers in the Citizen class, a special medal of achievement is awarded to those skiers who finish in a time no longer than 50 percent above the average of the five fastest skiers in their class. There are also awards for the top two skiers in each age classification as well as a team trophy to the fastest four-member team.

The second purpose of the circuit is to keep outstanding cross-country racers active after they have retired from national team activities. A Worldloppet champion will also be crowned each year. The champion will be determined by a point system. Challengers for this title must compete in at least six member races. One of these races must be in Scandinavia, one in North America, and one in Central Europe. The remainder of the races can be selected at will by the competitors. At the end of each racing season, skiers must send their passport to the Worldloppet secretary-general by the first of May to verify placement and time. The Worldloppet champion will then be determined and honored. A $1000 trophy will be presented to the winner.

What follows is my experience of this exciting event. Upon our arrival in Hull, Quebec, I was determined to try out my rusty high-school French on the first people I met. After spending two minutes trying out my broken French on a middle-aged couple at the motel, the gentleman turned to me and said, "Vee Svedes." That ended my attempts to appear bilingual, and I retreated to my room. I found out later that universal sign language can more than overcome any language barriers.

When we arrived at the Asticou Centre the next morning for the start of the race, my son Kevin and I were immediately aware that this was indeed a world-class event. The various flags from many nations around the world fluttered in the crisp morning air. The electronic timer was in place. A "spotter" helicopter landed in the field adjacent to the starting line, showering us with powder snow. The television and radio reporters were jockeying for position and ski manufacturers, clothing suppliers, and wax companies were trying to be as visible as possible. Kevin and I, along with other members of our racing team—the Chinguacousy Nordic Racing Team—felt that we were ready for our big test.

At the sound of the starter's gun, 1500 enthusiastic skiers took off. The six lanes of tracks were certainly helpful in easing the traffic flow although I felt as if we were involved in a game of roller derby on skis. Some skiers started as if they were involved in a five-kilometer sprint. After several skiers collided and wrestled each other to the ground, I knew that we were in for a long day.

After the first kilometer, we followed the Gatineau Parkway trail and a very long steep ascent toward Pink Lake. The altitude changes from 120 meters to 195 meters in a two-kilometer distance. When we reached the summit, the trail was relatively easy to checkpoint one. It was at this point I was grateful that I had waxed for grip rather than slip. It was also very obvious to me that I had vastly underestimated the difficulty of this course. After drinking a glass of honey mixture, I continued the trek.

The ascent continued up the Parkway trail to the twelve-kilometer mark where we encountered a very steep slope rising from 200 meters to 340 meters over a distance of only two kilometers. At this point, many skiers were showing signs of fatigue as the herringbone climbing technique was taking its toll. My wax was gripping extremely well as I passed many of the "herringboners" by walking straight up the extreme outside edges of these steep ascents. I had some difficulty when I strayed into loose-packed or powder snow so I decided to stay on the hard-packed surfaces wherever possible. The trails from this point on were only double tracked.

Although I was not gliding particularly well downhill, I felt fairly strong at this point in the race. I had managed to conserve energy on the uphills. I also rested in the tuck position when going downhill and concentrated on complete relaxation with deep breathing exercises.

At Huron Park Lodge checkpoint, the Swix company was offering to wax skis as an added service to the skiers. My wax was working to perfection so I declined their offer. The feeding station people here had Gatorade, water, a blueberry drink, chocolate chip cookies, and raisins. After a brief stop for ample liquids, I took off with renewed vigor and determination.

At about the twenty-one-kilometer mark from the departure point, the course reached its summit with an elevation of 350 meters. Here it became windy and very hilly. Many turns were located at the foot of hills. Because of the volume of skiers who had previously skied through this section, the hills had started to become icy and treacherous. Although each skier allowed five to ten seconds for the previous skier to start the descent down a steep pitch, every so often the lead skier would invariably fall. Because of the ice and the narrowness of the trail, a collision would inevitably occur and the trail would be blocked. Fortunately, I managed to avoid any disastrous incidents by skiing around a couple of trouble spots in the nick of time. Perhaps I was lucky. After the twenty-third kilometer, there was a fairly long and steep descent in the direction of the Fortune Parkway. I welcomed these long descents with a sense of relief as they enabled me to rest my arms and legs for the long uphills ahead.

At this point, I had established a steady rhythm and was skiing almost effortlessly using the double pole, single kick method, alternating with the diagonal stride.

After leaving checkpoint three, there is a steep descent toward Meech Lake. At the foot of the hill there is a sharp left turn, followed by a small bridge over the lake. After the bridge there is a small S-curve. I found it necessary to reduce my speed when nearing the small bridge in order to execute the S-turn.

The course continued with the crossing of Meech Lake's frozen surface. Here my troubles began. Since the lake is between two mountains, this area becomes bitterly cold, especially on a windy day. The cold winds off the lake made my face and hands extremely cold and the long, monotonous ski across the flats sapped my energy to a greater degree than I cared to admit at the time. I welcomed the fourth checkpoint and refueled for the next challenge that awaited me. Unfortunately, the cold winds encountered on the trip across the lake had chilled my muscles and made them stiffen up. To add to my misery, I now faced the most difficult section of the course. The altitude between the thirty-first and thirty-fifth kilometers rises from 180 meters to 340 meters. As I took nourishment, I asked one of the volunteers how many kilometers we had skied. She responded that I had reached the thirty-five-kilometer mark. I naturally assumed that I had a mere twenty kilometers to ski in order to reach my goal and capture that coveted medal. With hopes renewed and body replenished, I attacked the next elevation with dogged determination. Upon reaching the summit of that elevation five kilometers later (it felt more like ten kilometers), I was shocked to read a marker with "35 km" on it. It is impossible to describe the terrible letdown and mental fatigue that struck me at that moment. In my own mind, I had not progressed an inch!

It was at this point that I first entertained thoughts of quitting. My body was aching and my mind was beginning to wander. How was I ever going to ski another twenty kilometers to the finish? But then I thought of my son Kevin and the other members of the racing team of which I was a part. I thought of how far I had driven to reach this event and most of all I thought of the distance that I had skied thus far. There was no way I could quit. I was going to finish and I was going to finish in a good enough time to qualify for that medal.

The following five kilometers were skied over gradually rising terrain. I had to pace myself sensibly and keep something in reserve. Each kick was carefully executed so that I did not waste energy by slipping back. I concentrated on my technique and joined a "train" of four other skiers. I stayed with that train for the next ten kilometers. I let them pace me rather than trying to overtake them. I finally reached the forty-kilometer mark and the last checkpoint. I was racked with pain and starting to feel the cold. My speech was slightly slurred, although I was still in control of my faculties. I told a ski patroller of my difficulties and he suggested that I eat some food and take the time to have several drinks. Only fifteen kilometers to go, I kept repeating to myself. I knew that fifteen kilometers would feel like fifty kilometers.

Immediately upon leaving the last checkpoint my thumbs started to get very cold. Although I tried to pick up the pace, my thumbs became colder and a couple of fingers started to go numb.

My first thought was not to panic. I have had enough experience with cold and fatigue to realize that panic can be disastrous. I removed my pole straps from my wrists and on the follow-through from each single pole plant, I slapped my hands against the side of my legs. I increased my pace and developed a brand-new rhythm. On downhills I put both poles under one armpit and rubbed both hands together as well as rubbing them against my thighs. After skiing across a series of false plateaux, my hands were warm once again. I now had about eight kilometers left to ski and had joined a train of three other skiers. We encouraged one another to keep going and convinced each other that our times would qualify us for the medal. I soon realized that these three skiers had previously passed me at the Meech Lake checkpoint but had "hit the wall" at this stage in the race. One of them was barely moving forward on the long gradual inclines, but he was still making progress.

I soon left this group in their misery and concentrated on coping with my own. I forced myself to concentrate on every ski technique that I have used over the years. I even increased my pace by using the double pole, single kick method. I would kick with the left ski ten times in a row, then with the right ski and so on. I took turns resting my arms by letting them fall to the side and by relying solely on the diagonal stride. I rested my legs as my thighs began to knot up by double poling for long stretches at a time. I finally spotted a marker in the snow. It was the fifty-three-kilometer marker. I had only two kilometers to go. I couldn't believe it!

The adrenalin began to flow, I could taste victory; I knew that I had finally made it. I double poled down the final descent toward the Asticou Centre, skated around the final turn and headed into the straightaway toward the finishing gate. Although I was out on my feet, I flashed by several skiers as if I were on a cushion of air and lunged across the finish line like an Olympic champion to the cheers of the crowd. An official draped the achievement medal around my neck and congratulated me. Yes, indeed, I truly felt like an Olympic champion at that moment.

If the challenge of the Gatineau 55 appeals to you and you would like an entry form, write to: P.O. Box 69, Station "A", Ottawa, Ontario K1N 8V3.

Chapter Ten
Racing

WHEN THE SKIING SEASON IS OVER, there is no reason why you can't continue to maintain the high level of fitness that you earned on the trails during the winter months. Many skiers (including myself) like to relax a bit and enjoy themselves by participating in a number of summer activities including swimming, rowing, orienteering, and cycling. Other cross-country skiers enjoy long-distance running to maintain cardiovascular fitness and stamina. Although most skiers have different preferences as to their favorite off-season sports endeavors, most start roller skiing in the late summer to early fall at the latest. The important thing to remember is to stay active on a regular basis so that you will be ready for the first snowfall.

Shaping Up In The Off-Season

There have been many theories on how cross-country ski racers should train for their favorite sport after the snow melts. Some of the schedules set out by coaches for young racers are so intense and serious that before long the younger racer packs in the whole program.

My advice is to keep active by participating in a number of sports. It is best to take part in sports that offer specific exercises to improve your cross-country stamina, both cardiovascular and muscular. Sports that rank high for building cardiovascular fitness include cycling, orienteering, hill bounding, ski striding, running, and roller skiing.

For muscular fitness and upper body development, I would recommend rowing, roller skiing (double poling), and specific weight training on Universal equipment as well as on other available training gadgets such as the Exergenie. Concentrate on your individual weaknesses. We all have areas we should improve.

It is a known fact that the elite racers are at the top of their sport not only because of experience but also because of dedication to skiing-related exercises like roller skiing.

Many cross-country racers do not usually reach their peak until they are in their mid-to-late-twenties. Even though young racers may do the same amount of running, roller skiing, and hill bounding as veterans, it is unlikely that they will match the older skiers; not just yet. Younger skiers must be patient, for the time will come when all that dedicated training will pay off.

Above all else, I fully believe that you must enjoy whatever training endeavor you undertake. You don't have to experience intolerable pain to achieve a high level of fitness. It is far better to work out regularly at a reasonable pace, particularly in the early part of the off-season, than to "bust a gut" for one or two days and take two or three days off doing absolutely nothing.

Many racers, particularly the younger ones, slack off when it comes to off-season training. They think they can ski themselves into shape during the ski season. This simply won't work. The relatively short duration of the ski season makes it virtually impossible to reach peak form and peaking is absolutely necessary for competitive skiing.

Running and Related Exercises

Running is excellent for the cardiovascular system, but don't overdo it by running long distances while ignoring other muscle groups. You're not in training for the Boston Marathon. All skiers, particularly the older skiers, should concentrate initially on building endurance during the first two to three months of running. After this period, you should add interval workouts lasting two to three minutes. The intervals should be run at approximately 85 percent of your maximum heart rate (see the section on cardiovascular fitness in Chapter Three to calculate heart rate). Interval work will help you to attain fast contracting muscles with improved cardiovascular fitness.

Running workouts can take place anywhere. Ideally running on "soft" surfaces such as grass, an indoor or outdoor track, or the local conservation area is best because these surfaces are natural shock absorbers and save a great deal of wear and tear on the feet, ankles and knees. If time and location do not permit you to work on soft surfaces all the time, perhaps you can split your running time between the pavement and the conservation area. Speaking of conservation areas, why not join an orienteering club?

Orienteering

The sport of orienteering is really a running adventure. Rather than running around a track concentrating on pounding that hard pavement, orienteering offers something that keeps your mind occupied.

Orienteering, which takes place on a cross-country course, is a recognized Olympic sport combining decision making, endurance, speed, and navigational skills. Each competitor carries a map indicating a series of circled features that must be visited. The challenge is to find the fastest route between features. The person who completes the course in the fastest time wins. Besides being a lot of fun, it gives you a real workout from hill climbing to interval workouts and is a marvelous deviation from straight running. Why not contact a club in your area and discover for yourself the mental and physical rewards of orienteering?

Ski Bounding

Ski bounding is an uphill exercise using ski poles and simulating the skiing movement as closely as possible. The key to proper technique is to push off the ball of the leading foot with as much effort as possible, while reaching forward with the opposite arm (as you would in diagonal striding). The opposite foot lands on the ground in flat-footed style; immediately the weight rolls forward onto the ball of that foot, the skier springs forward, and so on.

Proceed slowly at first until you get the proper technique, remembering always to land flat-footed. This is essential if you are to derive the full benefit form ski bounding. Why? Because when you are snow skiing, that kicking foot is virtually flat against the snow in order to attain grip. As the hill becomes steeper and steeper, landing flat-footed will become increasingly difficult. As you near the top you will have no alternative but to land on the ball of the foot. As you get the feel of the technique I'm trying to describe, take the exercise one step farther and straighten the rear leg. The more you imagine that you are snow skiing the better your technique will become.

Try to find a very wide hill with varying heights, that is, a hill that slopes from a low level on one end to a higher level on the opposite end. Start doing loops up and down the hill at its lowest point with each loop leading to a steeper section of the hill. In order to measure your progress, devise a series of these loops, with each series containing ten or twelve loops. Begin by doing two or three series non-stop and build up from there, to ten or twelve series over a period of twelve to fourteen weeks.

Ski Striding

Ski striding is very similar to the striding or walking technique described in Chapter Three. Ski striding is different from ordinary striding because it should be practised on the hills and it emphasizes forward thrust off the appropriate leg by bending the ankle forward. Be careful not to bound or stride off a flat foot. By keeping the body rolling forward, you will be able to transfer your weight from the back of the foot to ball of the foot and will better simulate a good skiing technique.

Ski striding can be done while hiking or when you encounter a very long, steep uphill while distance running. Not only will ski striding keep you going, it will keep your cardiovascular system working at a very high rate.

Cycling

Cycling is an excellent form of exercise and provides a great change of pace from the running exercises. It is easier on the legs and ankles and, in fact, provides an excellent alternative to someone who may be recovering from a leg injury or is an injury-prone runner.

Cycling, particularly during long rides, gives you an opportunity to train yourself in proper feeding techniques while on the "fly." As in cross-country skiing, it is essential to replace liquids and food burned up by the body.

Cycling is also similar to cross-country skiing in that it requires a great deal of concentration. It is always necessary to scan the road ahead for bumps and ruts, to change gears as dictated by the terrain and to expend a high amount of energy on the uphills. Speaking of uphills, most racers stand up on them to simulate the motions used in skiing uphills. The ankles and hamstring muscles get a real workout, as does the cardiovascular system.

Roller Skiing

As I have covered some aspects of roller skiing in Chapter Three, I will reiterate some points previously made and add some new ones. Roller skiing, without doubt, better simulates on-snow skiing than any other sport. Ideally you have two pairs of roller skis if you can afford the extravagance. If not, you can choose between the two-wheeler or three-wheeler models.

The two-wheel models are faster and are ideal for practising the skating technique, as it is possible to "edge" the skis. Two-wheelers are also conducive to double poling on the flats. Double poling builds up the upper body and strengthens the arms. Another advantage with these models is that you can actually conduct turns and come to a complete stop on relatively short notice. The ability to stop is of prime importance on steep downhills. This sounds like the understatement of the year, doesn't it? Don't laugh, because with the three-wheel variety, it is virtually impossible to stop on short notice.

How do you stop on two-wheeler roller skis? You spread your legs as far apart as possible without being uncomfortable. Then you edge your skis inward while simultaneously forming an inverted "V" or snowplow position. Finally you place all your weight over your feet, lean forward and exert pressure on the inside "edges" by twisting your ankles inward. You then come to an uneventful stop. The verdict on two-wheel roller skis is that they are ideal for practising double poling techniques, perfect for skating, but weak for improving the diagonal stride (unless you ski a great number of hills).

The three-wheel skis (one in front, two in back) offer excellent control on the flats, are slower than the two-wheelers, but are ideal for simulating and strengthening your diagonal stride on the flats. Also, you can still hone and improve your double pole, single kick technique on them. The big disadvantage with three-wheelers is their poor turning and stopping capabilities.

Where should you roller ski? Seek out roadways that have a minimum of traffic. Be careful, don't take unnecessary chances and remember to think of your own safety at all times.

Roller skiing requires a great deal of concentration to make sure that your skis stay parallel to one another, or that you don't catch a pole on the tip of your skis. Once you fall, your concentration becomes even greater, because a fall on pavement is extremely painful and leaves permanent scars.

Roller skiing prepares your whole body for on-snow skiing. Your groin area will no longer hurt at the start of the season. Your double poling, through increased arm strength, will improve immensely. By concentrating on the uphills and using the diagonal stride, you will actually develop as strong a technique as you would during regular snow skiing. Most important, it is so easy to make the transition from dry land roller skiing to actual on-snow training. It is no exaggeration that you will be at least a month ahead of skiers who haven't done any roller skiing.

It all sounds so good, doesn't it? In fact, good things will happen—but don't get lazy. As roller skis have ratcheted wheels, you tend to forget the weighting and unweighting process. You'll have to concentrate on your kick and that all-important weight transfer to achieve the maximum benefit from roller skiing. Practise holding a glide for as long a time as possible. It's a wonderful test for your balance as well.

Muscular Fitness
How often have you seen strong runners with upper body physiques resembling toothpicks? Conversely, some body builders with bulging chests, arms, and thighs can hardly run.

Cross-country skiers resemble neither of these types. They must be strong, yet they must have speed and agility. They must develop a harmony of strength, speed, and coordination to attain that all-important commodity known as power.

There are different kinds of strength training. They include lifting barbells, and performing ski-related movements against resistance through the use of pulleys, armbands, and legbands.

As far as skiers are concerned, the old methods used, such as lifting heavy barbells with a few repetitions to build muscles, are obsolete. Homemade armbands, legbands, and pulleys have some use if no other equipment is available, but they have proven to be inadequate in the building of muscle endurance. (If you happen to live in the backwoods, chopping wood is great; but how many of us actually have a woodpile to chop? Homemade roller boards are fair, but you've got to be a carpenter to build a good one.)

Standing above all these gadgets and contraptions is one piece of equipment that can do it all for you: the Universal. These super gyms are found everywhere these days in health clubs, YMCA gyms, hotels, and schools. One single unit, a circuit training unit, allows you to do up to fourteen excellent variable resistance exercises. For example, you can develop strong arm and shoulder muscles using the shoulder press, chest press, high lateral pull, or chinning stations. For the legs, work out at the quad and leg curl or rowing stations. Strengthen the stomach muscles and back muscles at the abdominal and back hyperextension units respectively. There is a weight pulley station ideal for building those tricep muscles used in double poling. Do you want to increase the strength in the hamstring and quadricep muscles used for hill climbing? Use the thigh and knee extension station.

Set up a schedule of six to twelve exercises and work out three to five times a week. Perform the various exercises in sets. (If you perform one exercise ten times this is known as a "set.") Start slowly by doing one set each at five or six stations. By so doing you will get used to each apparatus and the weight that you are able to handle without too much strain. The number of sets can be increased gradually over a period of time. Don't forget to warm up with flexibility exercises: push-ups, sit-ups, twists, and even a few minutes on the stationary bike. Cool down in the same manner.

You will derive the greatest benefit from a steady training session with only short rest periods. At the end of your workout, you should be sweating and breathing somewhat more heavily than normal. Keep at it regularly, and in no time at all, you'll be more than ready to beat those hills to death.

On-Snow Training

When winter comes, your training program must be targeted so that you will peak just before the big races. Peaking occurs when you reach a point in your training schedule at which the recovery time after a hard training run is dramatically reduced. You feel that, even during your faster training runs, you could accelerate without any fear of exhausting yourself. You feel as if you could ski through the hills as if you were on the flats. You are light on your feet, even after diagonal striding up a particularly long uphill section. Your resting pulse is low and steady. To achieve this so-called "peak" condition, it is necessary to build from a base training program in a logical and predetermined manner.

Stamina is the watchword in cross-country skiing. Without it, you will never achieve your potential in either short- or long-distance events. At the start of the season, never start out by skiing at full speed as if you were in instant racing condition. The idea is to ski at a comfortable pace for increasingly long periods of time each time out in order to build up your level of cardiovascular fitness and to brush up on your technique.

Young skiers should not exceed a thirty- to forty-minute-workout. Older skiers should ultimately be able to ski for an hour or so. It is important to set up a training log in order to record your progress. As your progress is directly related to your pulse rate, it is important to stay within what I call your "TAG" or "talk and glide" limit. This means you should be able to carry on a brief conversation during your workout without sounding too breathless.

I would suggest that you set out on an intermediate, measured course and record the time that it takes you to complete it while staying within your TAG speed limit. When you feel that you are up to a greater challenge, change to a course with more hilly terrain and proceed in the same manner. Remember, your breathing and pulse will tell you whether to speed up or slow down and when to rest. Don't strain. It is far better to call it a day than to overdo it.

As in running, interval training is absolutely necessary if you are to cope with the pain associated with skiing fast for extended periods. Interval work gives your body the ability to recover from stressful workloads and prepares you for actual racing conditions. Through these workouts, you will learn how far and how hard you can push your body in competition. You will, in fact, develop a sixth sense that will tell you when to slow down or when to speed up.

The system of interval training that I adhere to allows me to train for both short- and long-distance races. I believe that it is best to combine interval work with leisurely skiing; that is, at a fast, then at a relatively slow pace.

I usually start out with a fairly short loop of five kilometers and ski it at or slightly above race pace. Rather than stop for a recovery rest, I stay on my skis and ski the loop again at a smooth leisurely pace. In other words, I use the second time around the loop as a recovery lap. I then repeat the process until my pulse and my body tell me to rest.

As mentioned in a previous chapter, I feel that it is unwise to be obsessed with the stop watch. I do, however, feel it is important to time your performance every so often in order to gauge your progress. As your TAG limit improves you should increase your workload by adding more laps per workout or by tackling a more difficult trail. By so doing, you are intensifying your training both in terms of effort and distance. It is also important to take on water every so often to avoid dehydration. Interval work should be done at least twice a week and should start at least four to five weeks before your event.

One area that is largely ignored by racers is the ability to ski at a steady pace uphill. In fact many races are won or lost on the uphill portions of the course. Hill training should become an integral part of your interval training workouts. Select a gradual uphill one or two kilometers in length and ski it as you would your normal interval loop. Repeat until you are tired. Hill training is also an excellent conditioner for the thigh muscles (quadriceps) as well as the hamstring muscles (muscles at the back of the leg).

Every hard training workout should be followed the next day by a steady, easy, long-distance ski to maintain and build on the stamina that you have already achieved. During those long-distance workouts, you should concentrate on your technique.

Racing Techniques

I have seen the best-conditioned athletes simply wear themselves out on the hills because they had poor technique. Poor technique or lack of technique means that you will be fighting yourself every inch of the way. Conservation of energy and easy, flowing skiing are the keys to becoming a competitive racer. It is a wise move to have a coach, an instructor, or even a fellow racer who is knowledgeable watch and analyze your style. Never be too proud to seek help and advice.

In my opinion North American skiers are every bit as fit as any athletes in the world; however, to date their technique has been inferior to that of the Russians, Norwegians, or Swedes.

You can be in top physical condition after months of training and you will still fall behind other skiers if you lack finesse.

Techniques for Flat Terrain

Many skiers try to copy other skiers who have a smooth stride pattern and who seem to glide over the snow in effortless fashion. To a point, it is beneficial to try to emulate a skier with good style. It doesn't matter how you look, however, as long as the kicking ski is in the right position for the downward-and-backward thrusting motion. The follow-through after the kick involves the pendulumlike, forward swing of the non-kicking leg and of the arm. The elite skiers kick down and back with power, but they also drive their opposite leg ahead at the same time with an equal amount of power. Without that forward leg power movement of the non-kicking ski, you will be a victim of "kick-skier only" syndrome, particularly in powder snow when the track could disintegrate at your feet. Always remember, power and lightness go together. A strong kick means nothing without the forward thrust of the non-kicking ski and arm. Be light, be quick, and be ready for the next kick from the opposite leg.

In cross-country ski racing, quickness is vital. Leg speed and arm coordination can mean the difference between finishing in the medals and being an also-ran. A fraction of a second in every forward leg-swing can be critical in a middle-or long-distance event. Stay light and quick.

Mechanics of the kick. The purpose of the kick is to get as much thrust along the track as possible without slipping backwards.

There are several factors that enter the picture here, such as snow conditions, timing, and waxing. In wet snow conditions where klister is used, only poor waxing will prevent you from having all the kick you need. If you have waxed properly for klister conditions, it is even possible to get away with a "late" kick. On hard packed powder snow, it is necessary to "weight down" the kicking ski much sooner. In these conditions, concentration and timing are the keys to attaining a proper kick. Don't forget to concentrate on that forward thrust of the non-kicking ski.

Regardless of your style, the lower leg of the kicking ski should be at a 90° angle to the snow. If the kick is a powerful one the leg will straighten out behind and then recoil slightly. If the kick is not powerful, the leg will not straighten and therefore the forward speed will be greatly reduced.

The arm swing and pole plant. Many skiers underestimate the value of the arms as a means of propulsion. In the last few years, long-distance runners have come to realize that you don't just run with the legs. As a result they have been concentrating on developing more upper body strength. The same principle applies to cross-country skiers.

In cross-country skiing, the arms should be used in much the same way as the legs. The pole should be planted at a point near the toe of the boot or slightly back of that point. The arm should be bent and ready for the push off. Downward and backward pressure is exerted on the pole the instant it hits the snow until the arm passes the hip. As in the kicking technique, follow-through is essential. The arm becomes fully extended and the grip is relaxed. Many skiers make a serious error in thinking that if they plant their poles farther ahead by reaching forward, their forward thrust will be greatly increased. Nothing could be farther from the truth. In fact, skiers who do this cannot use their poles at all until the glide permits. As a result, any momentum gained is lost before the poling action becomes effective.

The forward arm drive or swing takes place when the kicking foot is still in contact with the snow and provides both stability and body momentum. A strong arm swing also helps to propel the body forward.

Gliding position. It is obvious that the main purpose of the glide is to maintain forward momentum by capitalizing on a strong kick and poling action. To achieve maximum glide, the leg remains in a constant flex position when riding the glide ski. The weight is mainly on the heel with the lower part of the leg at a 90° angle to the ground. This keeps the ski tip light on the snow. All of the skier's weight remains on the gliding ski until the gliding leg loses contact with the snow when it finishes as the kicking leg.

Two serious errors that are quite common in gliding are straightening the glide leg and weighting the toe. Straightening the glide leg cuts off the glide prematurely and forces an earlier kick. Weighting the toe drives the ski into the ground and inhibits the glide. It takes a lot of energy to propel the body forward; don't waste it.

Double poling. There are two methods of double poling. Specifically, they are the no-kick, double pole and the single kick, double pole. A good racer must have a mastery of both methods.

The no-kick, double pole is mainly used in fast track conditions when the snow is hard packed. A short, rapid poling motion is used for propulsion. The hands reach back only as far as the hips and then swing up high to eye level. If you are to be successful at employing this technique, it is essential that you get as much of your body weight into the poling motion as possible. The arms should be slightly bent as you start your poling action. As the poles move to a position about even with the hips, lean down hard on the poles with your upper body and follow through with your hands and wrists. To achieve the full benefit from this downward-and-backward thrust, lean slightly back on your skis after the poling action. Make sure, however, that you are in the proper position to execute the next double pole action.

The single kick, double pole is used frequently in powder snow conditions and is more useful than the no kick, double pole in slower conditions. A more sweeping and powerful arm motion is used in this method, as there is a substantial extension of the legs. There is also added thrust because of the use of the legs.

The secret to mastering this technique is learning to swing one leg forward along with both arms. The forward leg thrust is very important here as well. (Accomplished racers lean out over their skis so far that only the pole plants with both arms fully extended prevent them from falling headlong into the snow.) The kicking ski is weighted down and pushed backward at the precise moment that the other leg is thrust forward. This action enables your skis to "catch up" to your poles to the point at which the arms can be bent for the pole push. The pole push should actually occur a split second after your kick. It will take constant practice to get the timing just right.

You must not develop the bad habit of always using the same ski to kick off. Practise with both the right and left foot with emphasis on your weak side. You will be glad that you can use either ski as the kicker when taking part in a long-distance event or when the kicking wax on one ski is not working as well as the wax on the other ski.

Maintaining momentum. Expert skiers will maintain a forward progressive speed no matter what terrain they face. Their all-round skills pay dividends when they come to S-turns and hairpin turns, or as they change from the skate to the double pole or single kick, double pole at a moment's notice. This reflex action is done without thinking, the result of hours of practice.

Remember to maintain that pendulum arm action even as you approach a turn or a series of turns. Ski as you would on a normal straight stretch and ski "through" the corners.

How to ski through tight turns. Suppose you have to turn a corner to the right. As you approach the turn, slide the left ski forward slightly ahead of the right ski and turn the right edge slightly into the track. Kick with the left ski and then bring the right ski along. As you come out of the turn and both feet come together, dig in the inside edge of the left ski and the outside edge of the right ski. The right ski now becomes the kicking ski. Hold your edges and follow-through with your normal kick and glide. The rule of thumb to follow is to always initiate your turn with the outside ski.

Another method of skiing the turns is to use shortened skating strokes. If you are skating around a right turn, the right ski should be in the right track. The stroking or skating ski (left ski) then propels you around the turn.

The Peaker Pump method. The skiing world has heard of the famous "Koch Kick;" now comes the "Peaker Pump." I'm not entirely sure if the skiing fraternity is ready for this one, because it makes a mockery of traditional techniques, but I have included the Peaker Pump here because it has worked so well for me in maintaining momentum in long-distance skiing on hard packed and icy tracks in particular.

This innovative method is used in conjunction with double poling and will propel you along icy tracks at unbelievable speeds. The concept is derived from the double pole, single kick method with a completely new twist. The single kick becomes a rapid-fire double, triple, or even quadruple kick. My method differs from the traditional double pole, single kick method in that the kicking ski never leaves the ground, and the gliding ski remains constant as the gliding ski. Of course, either the right or left ski can be used as the kicker. The legs work like scissors. The power from the hip is driven down the leg to the kicking ski. This power-packed motion drives both skis forward at an ever-increasing speed while a short, fast double poling action is maintained. The Pump can even be used when skiing up medium hills. Try it; it really works.

In the future, I can visualize one ski being waxed for glide and one ski waxed for kick. Theoretically this would make sense. Over a longer distance, however, the kicking leg would be built up to tremendous strength to carry such a heavy workload.

Uphill Technique

It's a known fact that racers spend more time on uphills during a race than anywhere else. It's the amount of time spent on climbing that separates the winners from the losers. In order to become proficient at climbing, racers must constantly practise their uphill technique and experiment with waxing ideas.

There are several techniques for climbing, with each technique varying according to the steepness of the ascent. In some cases, the herringbone may be used exclusively because of the steepness of the hill. Other hills may be easily negotiated with the double pole method. The ability to use different techniques for climbing will largely be determined by your physical condition and your level of expertise, but the wax you use will also dictate what technique you will use.

Gradua hills. On relatively gentle hills, the majority of good racers use the diagonal stride. Your body should be in a slightly lower position than it is when skiing the flats. Success will probably depend on extra weighting down of the kicking ski. This can be accomplished by exaggerating your lateral movement and increasing the flex in the kicking leg. Concentrate on getting extra thrust from the forward leg and by weighting down on it a split second earlier than normal. Maintain a strong arm thrust and ski through the hill. Always watch for nodules in the track and take advantage of them. They will help you kick and thereby speed up your ascent. A steady rhythm is essential. Perhaps you can also throw in some double poling for good measure if you have the necessary upper body strength.

Steep hills. Several terms have been used to describe different techniques for ascending steeper hills. I have heard of shuffling, bounding, running, and trolling. As I see it, however, you actually have two choices: a compacted version of the diagonal stride and the herringbone method. I use the herringbone only as a last resort.

Compact diagonal stride. As you approach a steep ascent, dramatically reduce your normal kick-and-glide length to short, fast, backward (on the kicking ski) and forward (on the glide ski) thrusts. Straighten up your body and get up on the balls of your feet. Lean into the hill and keep a very slight flex in the knees. Use your arm swing to lift up your body and plant the pole (or in the case of double poling, poles) directly beside your boot. Although this profile, with relatively stiff legs and straight body may seem awkward at first, stay with it. The idea is to use your hip power and body weight to generate downward thrust onto the kicking ski. Once that weight is on the kicking ski, the ankles and feet are used to exert downward and backward pressure. Remember your kicking leg is almost fully extended at the time of the kick.

The key move now is to weight down the kicking ski and to transfer all your weight to the opposite hip while leaning forward. The stiff kicking leg now becomes the lead ski leg or gliding ski. I hesitate to call it the gliding ski because very little gliding may be taking place because of the steepness of the incline. The lead leg should be kept stiff as well, because in a split second it will again become the "kicking" leg. Both hips remain in a "locked" position at all times. As you weight and unweight from side to side and develop a rhythm, you should almost develop a sense of weightlessness as you ascend the hill.

Herringbone method. When the track becomes broken down with the heavy traffic of preceding skiers, another technique must be used. The only one left, other than parallel side-stepping, is the good old herringbone.

If you are not on a nature hike but rather in a race, you'll want to move up the hill as fast as possible. The secret to executing the herringbone is to take short steps and to edge your skis just enough to keep them from slipping. Do not bend over too far; stay as upright as possible.

Although some instructors claim that you should use mainly the legs and not the arms in the herringbone, I strongly disagree. Some skiers have almost as much strength in their arms as in their legs. Proper use of the poles can have the same effect as fuel in a rocket launch. Use the poles to your advantage for that extra propulsion. Advising a skier not to use poles for the herringbone is like sending a wrestler into the ring with both hands tied behind his back.

Skating. Skating is now being used by some racers for the complete duration of both short and long-distance events. The long, rhythmic stroke of the marathon skate is being replaced by a new technique—a rapid, short, power-packed stroke.

This technique is now the center of great controversy as it is alleged that it is turning the sport into a freak show and taking the art and grace out of it. Some racers are using extremely short skis and very long poles to gain an advantage. Another complaint being made is that skating virtually annihilates groomed set tracks. I agree with both statements, but as long as this type of skating is allowed, a racer must be able to execute this technique properly to keep up with the competition. With this in mind, I advise any racer to develop skating abilities through on-snow practice, as well as in the off-season using roller skis.

I would also advise any racer not to abandon the traditional proven techniques in cross-country skiing, no matter what anyone says. I make this statement with the knowledge that at this very moment there is a movement afoot that skating be banned completely for all sanctioned cross-country ski races. Don't be surprised if a separate circuit is set up strictly for skating races. I know which event I will enter—how about you?

Downhill Technique

Throughout this book, I have emphasized that it is better to wax for grip rather than slip. I still believe that I am correct despite the latest emphasis on downhill waxing and de-emphasis on climbing waxes for the uphills. It is a fact that some of the slowest downhill skiers more than compensate for their lack of speed downhill by making up time on the uphill stretches and emerging victorious. I must admit, however, that you will never be a champion skier until your downhill techniques become respectable.

What does it take to be a good, fast downhill skier? Narrow skis with softer tips help because they are faster as they flex better with the nodules in the track. It also stands to reason that skis that are waxed with glide wax only will move faster than skis on which grip wax is used.

In terms of technique, good downhillers steer their skis carefully and avoid letting the tips and edges dig into the side of the track. They ride back on their skis, weighting their heels. They use their legs like pistons to ride the bumps smoothly with minimum effort. The fastest downhill skiers hold their tuck even over rough terrain, thereby reducing wind resistance dramatically.

You should use the downhills to relax and to replenish lost oxygen. Breathe slowly and deeply. If holding the tuck position is too difficult and begins to tire you out, simply rest your forearms on your thighs. This approach will still reduce wind resistance, and you will end up at the bottom of the hill refreshed.

Racing Advice

You have prepared yourself physically for the race through a training regimen that you felt was best for you. You feel ready for the big event both physically and mentally. There are many other factors, however, that should be taken into consideration at this time.

The course. Study a map of the course carefully and determine exactly the type of terrain it is that you will be encountering. For example, if the first ten kilometers are uphill, you would be a fool to start too fast. This would only result in "burn-out" before the race even started. Is the course hilly or flat? Is it a technically difficult course or an easy course? Develop your strategy around your strengths and weaknesses.

Waxing. How many times have you seen at least one or two skiers in an event at the side of the track waxing their skis after the event has started? It occurs in every race. There is no excuse for this. It is important to reach the race site at least one hour before the start of your event. Experiment with the wax that you think will work best for you. Ski at least four to five kilometers before making a final decision on wax selection. Once you have made a decision, stick with it and ignore any talk about waxing from other competitors. In other words, develop confidence in making your own decisions. I have already stressed in my waxing section that what works best for one skier may not work at all for another.

Mental outlook or psyching. A major factor in cross-country ski racing is mental outlook or attitude. Many good racers have lost the race before it even started because they have allowed themselves to be "psyched out."

Several years ago, my son Kevin, who had been skiing for four or five years, decided that he would like to become involved in cross-country ski racing. After entering and placing well in both time trials and other events he entered the regional provincial qualifying championships.

Upon our arrival at the race site both Kevin and I—his coach and mentor—were flabbergasted at the amount of sophisticated equipment that had been made available to his competitors. Being a one-man team from his local high school, Kevin was astounded to see other racers arriving in custom vans with team logos emblazoned on the sides. Further inspection showed that many of the team members had the latest racing skis and the most advanced binding systems that money could buy. Of course, they also had matching racing suits with the high school name on the front and back. To top it all off, these teams had coaches who waxed the racers' skis for them and who catered to their every need.

As registration was taking place inside the chalet, a number of "racers" surrounding Kevin were "strutting their stuff," talking about last year's champions, and boasting of their best times (naturally, greatly exaggerated). Kevin, upon hearing all the talk, was starting to become unglued—very nervous and apprehensive. It was at this time that I took him aside for a pep talk. I told him that I knew he was ready, and urged him to have confidence in his own abilities and to stay away from the other competitors. He took my advice.

As it was a very mild day (5° C) the other coaches were meticulously applying klister waxes with their hot irons to their protégés' skis.

Kevin felt that under the circumstances there was no way he would be competitive in view of the technology that was being exhibited by these "experts."

In direct contrast to the other coaches, I applied rough gobs of jackrabbit klister to Kevin's skis and corked it into each ski. I then applied a rough layer for extra grip. The other skiers, upon seeing what looked to be a mess of molasses and tar, laughed at our crude technique. Just before Kevin's start time my only words of advice were: "Do it." He nodded and said that he would.

In retrospect, I must admit that it was not Kevin who had been psyched out. Although I maintained an air of confidence, I honestly felt that he didn't stand a chance of placing.

At about five minutes from the anticipated finishing time, all the coaches, the media, and spectators started to crowd around the finish line.

The first skier to finish was the defending champion who had been the pre-race favorite. Two minutes later a skier in a red racing suit rounded the last corner. None of the coaches knew who he was as he approached the finish line. The unknown, unheralded skier was none other than my son Kevin. I let out an ear-shattering yell and threw my arms around him when he crossed the line. He had overcome long odds in qualifying for the provincial championships.

Pacing. Most young skiers, being naturally overexuberant, tend to ignore the importance of proper pacing. I also must blame many coaches who tell their young protégés to go all-out from start to finish. This is a senseless strategy and one that seldom works.

The secret to running a good race is to listen to your body. It will tell you when to speed up or when to slow down. Of course towards the end of any race you must force yourself to ignore some pain in order to finish strongly. If in a thirty-kilometer race you are exhausted at the fifteen-kilometer mark, however, you might as well forget about attaining a good result.

My philosophy has always been that it is far better to finish strongly than not to finish at all. To have a DNF (did not finish) after your name is far more embarrassing than finishing last, in my opinion.

If possible, stay with a train of skiers who are skiing at a pace at which you feel comfortable. Watch the other skiers in the train carefully and make your move past them one by one as they begin to falter. Move up to the rear of another train and let them pace you in the same manner.

If you are with the leading group of skiers, be careful that they are not setting too fast a pace and leading you down the trail to oblivion. It is very possible that most of this group will ultimately burn out towards the end of the race. By staying back a little, you will be able to take control of the race when they begin to falter. Some telltale signs of fatigue include: shakiness, labored breathing, sloppy, deteriorating style, slow arm swing, and lack of motivation on the uphills.

In cross-country skiing your goal in competition should be to develop the ability to ski at the necessary speed over the required distance without becoming completely exhausted. If you have a coach, he or she can give you split times in relation to other skiers at specific distances throughout the course. As you become more experienced, you will develop a timing mechanism in your head and will be able to estimate your time accurately to within a few seconds of your actual time.

Energy conservation through concentration and patience. From the start to finish of a race, conservation through concentration is critical. Many racers don't realize just how much energy they use up through poor pole plants, back slipping of the kicking ski, general scrambling for position, or just through poor judgment.

The most inefficient use of energy occurs at the start of a race. I have seen skiers literally sprint at the outset of a fifty-kilometer race, elbows flying, teeth gnashing, and poles spearing the skis and boots of fellow competitors. In many cases several skiers may even topple to the ground like wrestlers in a Texas Death match.

Some racers become so hyped up that if both tracks are occupied on a double tracked trail, they immediately jump into the powder snow off to one side and "snowshoe" it around to the front of the slower skiers. They obviously have never thought about the amount of energy they are expending by doing so. Be patient and call "track." In the end patience will save you both time and energy: two valuable commodities in cross-country ski racing.

Even as fatigue sets in, it is essential to concentrate on your kick and on your overall style. If you don't, you'll get overtired and depressed.

Energy conservation through alertness. Cross-country skiing requires brawn. A skier who is all brawn and no brains, however, won't progress very far up the ladder. Good skiers will look ahead at the turns and will skate around corners whenever possible to save fractions of seconds. They use small bumps in the track to accelerate the thrust of their kick. Well-balanced racers will break into a full skate in open sections where there are no tracks or where conditions indicate that skating would be advantageous.

The intangibles. The sports world has seen many athletes who did not have any natural ability rise to the pinnacle of success. They did possess, however, an insatiable desire to be the best and were willing to sacrifice anything to achieve their goal. They are called "the Grinders." The grinders (or dark horses of the sports world) emerge victorious because they have extra "heart"—and a burning desire to succeed. You can have all the natural ability in the world but without drive and heart it just won't happen.

Chapter Eleven

Happiness is Spring Skiing

MANY SKIERS LOOK OUT their windows in the city and upon seeing bare pavement and green grass, they assume that skiing is *tout fini* for the season. Unfortunately these people are missing out on what I feel is the best time of year for cross-country skiing. They are missing the exquisite joys of spring skiing.

The snow may be beginning to disappear like melting ice cream on a hot summer day, but a little farther, in the bush, there is an abundance of white stuff left as a result of the constant grooming and packing of trails during the winter months. In many areas a base of sixty to seventy centimeters remains on the trails, and neither rain nor warm weather is going to make it disappear overnight. There may be the odd bare spot, but you shouldn't let that stop you.

At the writing of this section of the book, I had just returned from a wonderful outing at one of the local conservation areas. I had left very early in the morning and had experienced two completely different skiing conditions in one day.

On my arrival the groomed tracks had been frozen to a glaze overnight—perfect conditions for a fast workout. I was completely alone with the smells and sounds of spring. The birds were chirping, and the streams were bursting out over their banks. The waterfalls at the various dams sounded like miniature generating stations. The maple trees were being tapped for maple syrup. My adrenalin started to flow.

After I laced on a generous portion of jackrabbit klister wax, I was about to start out when I heard what I thought was a very loud barking sound. When I looked up into the sky, however, I soon realized that the "barking" came from a gaggle of Canada geese, huge birds winging their way across the sky. I asked myself, "Where are all you skiers?" Then I suddenly felt greedy and smug. I had the ski trails all to myself. I wouldn't have to share them with anyone on this beautiful spring morning. For once I wouldn't have to yell "track" or stop to lend waxing assistance to novices. For a moment I selfishly thought that I should keep these perfect conditions secret from the world.

I suddenly awoke from my thoughts and took off like a jack-rabbit. I glided over the tracks like a speed skater, my wax working to perfection. I felt like I could beat Pierre Harvey and Bill Kock with both hands tied behind my back. The crusty, slick trails were perfect for the diagonal stride, for skating, for double poling and ideal for the "Peaker Pump." Even the downhills were faster than I had ever seen them. As I rounded one hairpin turn at high speed while holding my tuck position, I imagined that I was Ken Read or Franz Klammer competing in a World Cup downhill event. What a feeling!

Alas, like Cinderella, the bubble was soon to burst for me. As the sun grew stronger and the snow began to warm up, I gradually started to feel myself slow down. Mother Nature was changing me from a "world class" racer to an average tourer, and there was nothing I could do but accept it. Now was the time to absorb nature at its best, to feel the warmth of the earth and to devour the sights and sounds around me.

I was about to retire for the day when another spring skiing fanatic appeared out of nowhere. It was my longtime friend and skiing companion André Ouimet. He let loose with his customary yodel and off we went together.

An excellent skier and racer, André opened up a whole new dimension in spring skiing to me on that particular day. After noticing that the tracks were becoming very soft, he suddenly veered off the trail into the bush. I wasn't sure just what his intentions were when he disappeared from sight. A moment later

I caught a glance of him skating gracefully on the crust beside the dilapidated tracks. He was literally dancing around the trees, ducking overhead branches and hopping over exposed rocks and bare patches. He was Jean-Claude Killy and Jackrabbit Johannsen rolled into one. It was a virtuoso performance—one even Jackrabbit himself would applaud.

As I continued on my way along the trail, I suddenly thought that I was seeing a mirage. There appeared to be a fisherman sitting on a bridge. I couldn't believe my eyes! As I skied across the bridge on a narrow ribbon of snow that remained, the fisherman looked at me as if I had just arrived from outer space.

Undaunted, I continued my trek. Suddenly I ran out of track and there appeared ahead of me a gurgling stream that rushed across the trail. The previously frozen brook had fallen victim to the spring thaw too and had been transformed into a miniature lake.

At this point I had already covered approximately fifteen kilometers, and although I entertained thoughts of retracing my tracks, I decided to complete my run at any cost. I removed my skis, boots, and socks and rolled up my pant legs. As I waded into the knee-deep water carrying poles, skis, and boots, I slipped slightly and lost one ski. It was quickly gobbled up by the current and swept downstream—without its owner attached.

Although my first instinct was to curse my bad luck, I had to laugh at what must have been a very funny sight. After some struggling, I finally caught up with my wandering ski and scrambled out of the water. It was at this very moment that an older couple, who were walking their dog, appeared on the scene. They laughed with such gusto that their knees almost buckled. I laughed with them, as well as at their parting words: "We've seen some sights, but this is a first."

Feeling as totally refreshed as if I had taken a cold shower, I got all my gear back on and continued on my way. The balance of the trail was still well preserved and covered with snow, so I arrived at the trail's end without any other serious challenges. The experiences of that day will be savored forever in the back of my mind. Try it yourself; you'll like it!

Part Four
Practising Your Skiing Skills

Where to Ski in Canada

Chapter Twelve
Where to Ski in Canada

CANADA'S VAST LANDSCAPE offers virtually unlimited opportunities to indulge in the joys of cross-country skiing. This comprehensive guide covers the country from ocean to ocean, province by province, in a concise and easy-to-follow manner. The preface to each provincial listing indicates the topography, climate, and points of interest. Whether you are planning a day trip or an extended vacation, there is a ski area or resort ready to welcome you somewhere in Canada.

Although every effort has been made to gather together a comprehensive list of Canadian cross-country resorts, it is inevitable that I have failed to mention some areas. I apologize for any such omissions and trust that those resorts will contact their respective provincial authorities in order to ensure that they will be listed in future brochures and promotional materials.

Newfoundland and Labrador

Although Newfoundland is probably best known for its fishing industry, its ample forests have proven to be one of the province's most valuable assets. Newfoundland is a picturesque place to visit, and although cross-country skiing is not a large participatory sport to date, it is growing in popularity there.

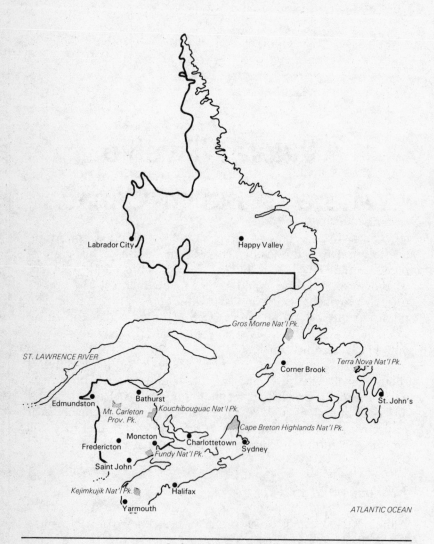

Labrador City

Happy Valley

Gros Morne Nat'l Pk.

ST. LAWRENCE RIVER

Corner Brook

Terra Nova Nat'l Pk.

St. John's

Edmundston

Bathurst

Mt. Carleton Prov. Pk.

Kouchibouguac Nat'l Pk.

Moncton

Charlottetown

Cape Breton Highlands Nat'l Pk.

Fredericton

Fundy Nat'l Pk.

Sydney

Saint John

Kejimkujik Nat'l Pk.

Halifax

Yarmouth

ATLANTIC OCEAN

Atlantic Provinces

Numerous waterfalls and rapids highlight the landscape, particularly where the streams of the western highlands drop steeply to the coast. Rock basin lakes punctuate the terrain and add to the province's beauty.

The future development of Labrador's great forests will not only be of great benefit economically to the province, but will also expand its recreational facilities, including those geared towards cross-country skiing.

For more information about cross-country skiing in Newfoundland, contact:

Peter Cleary
Come By Chance
Newfoundland A1B 1N0
(709) 542-3259

Prince Edward Island

"The Garden Province" (or "The Million Acre Farm" as it is sometimes called) is part of the great synclinal lowland called the Maritime basin. The native people's name for Prince Edward Island was *Abegweit* which means "cradled on the waves." None of Prince Edward Island is more than 150 meters above sea level but it has a lovely, rolling countryside accentuated by beautiful red cliffs.

Is it any wonder that both tourists and locals flock in ever-increasing numbers to the numerous provincial parks to enjoy the natural winter beauty to the fullest? With over one hundred kilometers of skiing trails to choose from in the four primary areas—Brudenell, Brookvale, Mill River Park, and Prince Edward Island National Park—it is no surprise to learn that skiing is enjoying unprecedented popularity in beautiful Prince Edward Island. In addition to these public areas, there are many semi-public ski trails that traverse old logging and farm roads. These form local networks in and around Tyne Valley, Victoria, Belfast, Rollo Bay, and Grand Tracadie.

For more information about cross-country skiing in Prince Edward Island, contact:

Ulysses Robichaud
RR1, Hunter River
Prince Edward Island C0A 1N0
(902) 964-2193

Nova Scotia

Nova Scotia is physically and culturally diverse. Three distinguishable regions are: Northern Nova Scotia (including the Annapolis Valley), the Atlantic Upland and Eastern Shore, and Cape Breton Island.

Indelibly etched in the minds of many cross-country skiers is the experience of skiing at the Cape Breton Highlands Provincial Park. This beautiful park is skirted by the famous Cabot Trail which winds its way past some of the most rugged coastal country in eastern North America.

For more information about cross-country skiing in Nova Scotia, contact:

Nordic Ski Nova Scotia
Box 3101, Postal Station South
Halifax, Nova Scotia B3J 3G6
(902) 425-5450

New Brunswick

The natural beauty of New Brunswick is reflected by the fact that about 75 percent of the total land area is forested. Nowhere in eastern North America are there more magnificent red and white pines.

New Brunswick's rolling, thickly forested landscape, rimmed on three sides by the sea and divided up by such great rivers as the Saint John, "Canada's Rhine," offers cross-country skiers some of the most picturesque, varied terrain in Canada. It is no wonder that skiing is a thriving sport in this province; the scenery is unbeatable. Most of the national parks offer groomed trails.

For more information about cross-country skiing in New Brunswick, contact:

Mike Lushington
Box 9, Site 11
Balmoral, New Brunswick
E0B 1C0
(506) 826-3083

Newfoundland and Labrador

Name, Address and Telephone	Tracks Groomed or Machine Set	Ungroomed	Gear Rentals Yes	No	Instruction Yes	No	Lodging Yes	No	Other
Birchbrook Nordic Ski Club* Box 386, Station C Happy Valley/Goose Bay A0P 1C0 (709) 896-5074	30 km	unlimited	X		X			X	
Blow-Me-Down Ski Club* 31 Raymond Heights Corner Brook A2H 2S2 (709) 634-4967	8 km	over 100 km	X		X			X	
Clarenville Ski Club* Box 532 Clarenville A0E 1J0 (709) 466-7807	10 km	45 km	X		X			X	Lodging nearby. Backpacking, wilderness skiing.
Menihek Nordic Ski Club Box 38 Labrador City A2V 2L8	over 50 km	unlimited	X		X			X	High-performance training centre. Night skiing; spring skiing.
St. John's Cross-Country Ski Club Box 7201 St. John's A1E 3Y4 (709) 726-8876	2 km	over 50 km	X		X			X	Night skiing.

*Cross-country skiing events are held at these locations.

Prince Edward Island

Name, Address and Telephone	Tracks Groomed or Machine Set	Ungroomed	Gear Rentals Yes	No	Instruction Yes	No	Lodging Yes	No	Other
Brookvale Ski Park 10 km north of Crapaud on Hwy 13 (902) 658-2925	17.5 km		X			X		X	Tobogganing.
Brudenell River Park 5 km west of Georgetown (902) 652-2356	17.5 km		X			X		X	Tobogganing. Kitchen shelter for outdoor winter cooking.
Mill River Park 13 km south of Alberton (902) 859-2448	14.5 km		X			X		X	
Prince Edward Island National Park Box 487, Charlottetown C1A 7L1 (902) 672-2211				X		X		X	Snowshoeing, ice skating.

Nova Scotia

Name, Address and Telephone	Tracks Groomed or Machine Set	Ungroomed	Gear Rentals Yes	No	Instruction Yes	No	Lodging Yes	No	Other
Beaver Mountain Park (Antigonish)	4 km			X		X		X	
Beech Brook Lodge (Windsor) Take exit #3 off Hwy 101, travel 12 miles west on Hwy 1 (902) 757-2211	10 km		X		X			X	Guided trips. Warming shelters.
Cape Breton Highlands National Park Ingonish Beach Cape Breton B0C 1L0 (902) 285-2691	55 km		X			X		X	Warming shelters.
Dalhousie Mountain Recreation Ski Area Hwy 4, Glen Road Pictou County	12 km		X			X		X	
Highland Ski Touring RR 2, Cape North Cape Breton B0C 1C0 (902) 383-2952	5 km		X			X		X	Guided trips.
Kejimkujik National Park Maitland Bridge Annapolis County B0T 1N0 (902) 242-2770	47 km		X			X		X	

Name, Address and Telephone	Tracks Groomed or Machine Set	Ungroomed	Gear Rentals Yes	No	Instruction Yes	No	Lodging Yes	No	Other
Normaway Inn Margaree Valley Cape Breton B0E 2C0 (902) 248-2987	20 km		X		X		X		Guided trips.
Old Orchard Inn Ski Touring Centre* Box 1090 Wolfville B0P 1X0	20 km		X		X		X		Telemarking. Ice skating, indoor pool, sauna.
Vie Island Park Economy B0M 1J0	6.5 km			X		X		X	
Wentworth Hostel Hwy 104, Wentworth Centre Cumberland County B0M 1Z0 (902) 548-2379	70 km		X				X		

*Cross-country skiing events are held at these locations.

New Brunswick

Name, Address and Telephone	Tracks Groomed or Machine Set	Ungroomed	Gear Rentals Yes	No	Instruction Yes	No	Lodging Yes	No	Other
Les Aventuriers Ski Club* Charlo E0B 1M0 (506) 684-4497	43 km		X			X		X	
Fundy National Park Box 40 Alma E0A 1B0 (506) 887-2000		90 km	X		X		X		Lodging nearby. Ice skating, snowshoeing, tobogganing, snowmobiling.
Kouchibouguac National Park* Kouchibouguac E0A 2A0 (506) 876-2443	25 km	10 km	X			X		X	Gear rental nearby. Lodging nearby. Tobogganing. Nature guides available.
Mactaquac Park Mouth of Keswick E0H 1N0 (506) 454-6031	80 km			X		X		X	Lodging nearby. Horsedrawn sleigh rides, tobogganing.
Sugarloaf Provincial Park* Box 639 Campbellton E3N 3H1 (506) 753-6258	20 km		X		X			X	Lodging nearby. Alpine skiing, tobogganing.

*Cross-country skiing events are held at these locations.

HUDSON BAY

JAMES BAY

Port-Cartier Sept-Iles Pk.

Sept-Iles

ST. LAWRENCE RIVER

Gaspesian Pk.

Gaspé

Laurentide Pk.

OTTAWA RIVER

Mont Tremblant Pk.

Gatineau Pk.

Quebec

Hull

Montreal

Quebec

Quebec

La belle province is the epitome of elegance when it comes to cross-country skiing. Quebec has a reputation for excellent natural snow conditions and a prolonged ski season that lasts from November right into late April. As my hero Jackrabbit Johannsen discovered many years ago, the Laurentians, located just an hour or two by car north of Montreal, provide some of the best cross-country skiing in North America. It's easy to imagine that you are skiing in the French Alps or Switzerland rather than on the North American continent. With thirty major ski centers in a sixty-kilometer radius, there is a terrain to suit every taste. For those die-hards who just can't get enough skiing, there are several resorts in the Piedmont/Val Morin/Saint-Sauveur/Mont-Rolland area that feature night skiing.

One outstanding example of the availability of excellent cross-country skiing combined with first-class accommodation is the Far Hills Inn, located at Val Morin, just eighty kilometers north of Montreal. This fabulous seventy-five-room mountain-top resort offers an outstanding network (125 kilometers) on terrain of unsurpassed beauty including the Maple Leaf East Trail. Ski weeks include daily guided touring with instruction.

The Laurentians, part of the oldest mountain chain in the world, are truly impressive. Once visited, they are never forgotten. This is what makes Quebec the choice of so many cross-country skiers for their skiing holidays.

For more information on cross-country skiing in Quebec, contact:

La Fédération Québécoise de Ski
4545 Avenue Pierre-de-Coubertin
Box 1000, Station M
Montreal, Quebec H1V 3R2
(514) 252-3000, ext. 3565

Quebec

Name, Address and Telephone	Tracks Groomed or Machine Set	Tracks Ungroomed	Gear Rentals Yes	Gear Rentals No	Instruction Yes	Instruction No	Lodging Yes	Lodging No	Other
Alpin Inn* Ste. Marguerite Station JOT 2K0 1-800 363-2577			X			X	X		Indoor pool, indoor skating rink.
Auberge La Boule* Lac Carre JOT 1J0 (819) 688-2503		50 km	X			X	X		Sauna, ice skating, tobogganing, hay rides, nature trips.
Auberge Les Quatre Temps* Box 723 Lac Beauport G0A 2C0 (418) 849-4486	80 km		X		X				Ice skating, snowshoeing.
Auberge Noroit* Lac Superieur JOT 1P0 (819) 688-2503		50 km	X			X	X		Sauna, ice skating, hay rides.
La Bal du Plein Aire Estcourt G0L 1J0 (418) 859-2405	60 km		X		X		X		Guided tours. Telemarking. Snowshoeing.
Centre de Ski de Fond Mont Sainte Marie Lac Sainte Marie J0X 1Z0 (819) 467-5200	30 km		X		X		X		Sauna, whirlpool, sleigh rides. Guides available.

Name, Address and Telephone	Tracks Groomed or Machine Set	Ungroomed	Gear Rentals Yes	No	Instruction Yes	No	Lodging Yes	No	Other
Centre de Ski de Fond 612 Rue du Village Morin Heights JOR 1HO (514) 226-2417				X		X		X	Group ski tours by reservation.
Centre Touristique de la Petit Rouge St-Emile de Suffolk JOV 1YO (819) 426-2191	40 km			X		X		X	Guided tours.
Chateau Beauvallon* Box 138 Mont Tremblant JOT 1ZO (819) 425-7275			X			X		X	Gear rentals nearby.
Le Chateau Montebello Montebello JOV 1LO (819) 423-6341	100 km		X			X	X		Ice skating, sledding, racquetball & pool.
Far Hills Inn Val Morin JOT 2RO Montreal: (514) 866-2219 Val Morin: (819) 322-2014	80 km		X			X	X		Indoor pool, sauna, indoor tennis nearby.
Farmer's Rest* RR 4 Sutton JOE 2KO (514) 243-5224	43 km		X			X		X	Lodging nearby. Telemarking.

Name, Address and Telephone	Tracks Groomed or Machine Set	Ungroomed	Gear Rentals Yes	No	Instruction Yes	No	Lodging Yes	No	Other
Gray Rocks Box 1000 St-Jovite J0T 2H0 (514) 228-2571	30 km		X		X		X		Hut-to-hut touring. Skating, sleigh rides, sauna.
Hotel L'Esterel Box 38 Ville d'Esterel J0T 1E0 (514) 228-2571	50 km		X		X		X		Night skiing. Indoor pool, sauna.
Laketree Ski Lodge RR 2 Knowlton J0E 1V0 (514) 243-6604	90 km		X		X		X		Gear rentals nearby. Instruction nearby. Ice skating.
La Refuge 1186 Edmond Street St-Adolphe Stoneham G0A 4P0 (418) 848-3329 694-9213	220 km		X		X		X		Instruction nearby. Lodging nearby. Sledding.
Villa Bellevue Mont Tremblant J0T 1Z0 (819) 425-2734	90 km		X		X		X		Telemarking. Alpine skiing.

*Cross-country skiing events are held at these locations.

Ontario

The province of Ontario has virtually unlimited cross-country possibilities. The incredible variety of trails and terrains from Windsor to the Quebec border offers limitless opportunities for every class of Nordic skier. Cross-country skiing can be enjoyed throughout the province as well on local golf courses, parks, ravines, and even at the Metro Zoo on the outskirts of Toronto, where wildlife can be seen in abundance.

Travel west to the scenic shores of Lake Huron and ski at the Pinery Provincial Park, or take a slide on the boards while at the park at Niagara Falls.

Drive east along the St. Lawrence and Ottawa Rivers and you will find hundreds of kilometers of groomed trails for your skiing pleasure. Accommodations range from rustic to luxurious. Take your pick and enjoy.

In Southern Ontario, you can be ''pampered'' in the traditional snowbelt areas such as Muskoka, Haliburton, the Bruce Peninsula, the Kawarthas, or Huronia. These areas offer fabulous skiing by day and luxurious surroundings at night. A couple of outstanding resorts are the Pinestone Inn and the Maple Sands Resort in Haliburton. In the Muskoka area, the Deerhurst Inn is attracting international attention.

For heartier souls who prefer to live in harmony with the wilderness for a few days, I would recommend the seclusion of Algonquin Park. This area, known as Ontario's near-north, is internationally recognized as one of North America's best Nordic ski areas. The marked trails, some of which are groomed, cut deep into the heart of Algonquin.

The avid, adventuresome skier can even enjoy the exhilaration of hut-to-hut skiing and can tour for days through spectacular forests under the direction of a guide. One need not be an expert in order to appreciate this unique experience as the well-equipped huts are spaced approximately fifteen kilometers apart.

Farther north in the North Bay and Mattawa area, you will find over 150 kilometers of marked and groomed trails. In the Temagami region, famous for its lakes, a ski touring package is offered whereby you can ski from lodge to lodge. The rugged day's skiing activities are tempered by the relaxed and comfortable amenities of the lodges at night. Lodge-to-lodge skiing is designed to accommodate all levels of skiers.

Ontario

A unique experience can be had in Algoma country, north of Sault Ste. Marie, where elevation changes of hundreds of meters in less than four kilometers provide a spectacular view of virgin territory.

For more information on cross-country skiing in Ontario, contact:

Janet Rutka (Southern Ontario)
Box 7400, Station B
Willowdale, Ontario M2K 2R6
(416) 495-.210
or
Kitty Dustin (Northern Ontario)
176 Old Garden River Road
Sault Ste. Marie, Ontario P6B 5A6
(705) 253-6407

Northern Ontario

Name, Address and Telephone	Tracks Groomed or Machine Set	Ungroomed	Gear Rentals Yes No	Instruction Yes No	Lodging Yes No	Other
Ahmic Lake Resort Box 18 Ahmic Harbour P0A 1A0 (705) 387-3853	7 km		X	X	X	
Airport Ski Trail Box 1160 Wawa P0S 1K0 (705) 856-2396	11 km		X	X	X	Lodging nearby.
Beaubien Lake Trail Box 5080 Kenora P9N 3X9 (807) 468-9841	20 km		X	X	X	Cookout shelter. Warming huts.
Cambrian College Ski Trails 1400 Barrydowne Road Sudbury P3A 3V8 (705) 566-8101 Ext. 291	5 km		X	X	X	Lodging nearby.
Camp Can-USA Lodge Group Box 1, Island #212 Temagami P0H 2H0 (705) 237-8965	4 km access to Temagami trail system		X	X	X	

Name, Address and Telephone	Tracks Groomed or Machine Set	Ungroomed	Gear Rentals Yes No	Instruction Yes No	Lodging Yes No	Other
Camp Conewango Cross-Country Ski Centre RR2 Redbridge POH 2AO (705) 776-2320	260 km	200 km	X	X	X	3 km lighted trail. Dining room, snack bar.
Camp Manito Hotel Box 4, Island #205 Temagami POH 2HO (705) 237-8933	4 km access to Temagami trail system		X	X	X	
Candy Mountain Resorts Ltd. Box 367 Thunder Bay P7C 4V9 (807) 939-6033	10 km		X	X	X	Lodging nearby. Warming huts. Coffee shop.
Caswell Resort Box 70 Sundridge POA 1ZO (705) 384-5371	18 km		X	X	X	Indoor pool, sauna.
Centennial Park 950 Memorial Avenue Thunder Bay P7B 4A2 (807) 683-6511	17 km		X	X	X	Lodging nearby. Snack bar, lunch room. Nightly sleigh rides.
Chapleau Ski Club Box 885 Chapleau POM 1KO (705) 864-0707	15 km		X	X	X	Lodging nearby. Snack bar. Warming hut.

Name, Address and Telephone	Tracks Groomed or Machine Set	Ungroomed	Gear Rentals Yes	No	Instruction Yes	No	Lodging Yes	No	Other
Deep River Cross-Country Ski Club Box 999 Deep River K0J 1P0 (613) 584-2565	15 km	160 km	X		X		X		Lodging nearby. Warming huts. One lighted trail of 0.7 km.
Dryden Ski Club Box 25 Dryden P8N 2Y7 (807) 223-4291	35 km		X		X			X	Snack bar, lunch room.
Forest Lea Cross-Country Ski Trail Box 220 Pembroke K8A 6X4 (613) 732-3661	14 km		X		X			X	
Fort Creek Conservation Area Sault Ste. Marie Region Conservation Authority 99 Foster Drive Sault Ste. Marie P6A 5X6 (705) 949-9111	6 km		X		X		X		Lodging nearby.
Geraldton Cross-Country Ski Club Box 523 Geraldton P0T 1M0 (807) 854-0130	80 km	30 km	X	X	X		X		Lodging nearby.

Name, Address and Telephone	Tracks: Groomed or Machine Set	Ungroomed	Gear Rentals Yes	No	Instruction Yes	No	Lodging Yes	No	Other
Hearst Cross-Country Ski Club Box 2687 Hearst P0L 1N0 (705) 362-4346	26 km			X		X		X	Lodging nearby. Warming huts.
Hiawatha Lodge II – Kinsmen Park RR 5 Sault Ste. Marie P6A 6J8 (705) 949-9757	30 km		X		X			X	2 km lighted trail. Sauna.
Idylwylde Golf And Country Club 400 Walford Road East Sudbury P3E 2G9 (705) 522-8580	6 km						X		Snack bar.
Kakabeka Falls Provincial Park Box 5000 Thunder Bay P7C 5G6 (807) 475-1531	15 km	12 km	X		X			X	Lodging nearby.
Kamiskotia Ski Resort 300 Toke Street Timmins P4N 6V5 (705) 268-9057	7 km		X		X			X	Lodging nearby. Dining room, snack bar.
Kamview Ski Area Box 5000 Thunder Bay P7C 5G6 (807) 475-1531	21 km		X		X			X	Lodging nearby.

Name, Address and Telephone	Tracks Groomed or Machine Set	Ungroomed	Gear Rentals Yes	No	Instruction Yes	No	Lodging Yes	No	Other
Kap-Kig-Iwan Provincial Park Box 520 Englehart POJ 1H0 (705) 544-2331	6 km			X		X		X	Lodging nearby. Warming huts.
Kap Sno Rovers Club Box 123 Kapuskasing P5N 2Y3 (705) 335-2110	10 km double tracked			X		X		X	Lodging nearby.
Ket-Chun-Eny Lodge Group Box 7 Temagami P0H 2H0 (705) 237-8952		Access to Temagami trail system	X			X		X	
Kettle Lakes Provincial Park 896 Riverside Drive Timmins P4N 3W2 (705) 267-7951	18 km			X		X	X		Warming huts.
Kwagama Lake Lodge 176 Manitou Drive Sault Ste. Marie P6B 5L1 (705) 253-3075	75 km			X		X		X	Cookout shelter. Warming huts. Sauna.
Lake Herridge Lodge RR 1 Temagami P0H 2H0 (705) 569-3718	22 km			X		X		X	Outdoor curling, toboggan slide.

Name, Address and Telephone	Tracks Groomed or Machine Set	Ungroomed	Gear Rentals Yes	No	Instruction Yes	No	Lodging Yes	No	Other
Lake Laurentian Conservation Area Nickel District Conservation Authority 200 Brady Street Sudbury P3E 5K3 (705) 674-5249	16 km			X		X		X	Lodging nearby. Snack bar, lunch room. Warming huts.
Larder Lake Ski Club Box 196 Larder Lake P0K 1L0 (705) 643-2770	10 km			X		X		X	Lodging nearby. Snack bar. Warming huts.
Laurentian University Ski Trails Ramsey Lake Road Sudbury P3E 2C6 (705) 675-1151	15 km	15 km	X		X			X	Lodging nearby. Warming huts. Indoor pool, sauna.
Les Feux Follets 110 Morin Field P0H 1M0 (705) 758-6711	16 km			X		X		X	Lodging nearby. Snack bar, lunch room.
Limberlost Lodge RR 3 Thessalon P0R 1L0 (705) 841-2231	18 km			X		X		X	Sauna.
Loney's Sportsman's Lodge Box 475 Garson P0M 1V0 (705) 858-1281	60 km		X			X		X	Cookout shelter. Sauna.

Name, Address and Telephone	Tracks Groomed or Machine Set	Ungroomed	Gear Rentals Yes	No	Instruction Yes	No	Lodging Yes	No	Other
Marten River Provincial Park Marten River P0H 1T0 (705) 474-5550	11 km			X		X		X	Lodging nearby.
Mount Evergreen Ski Club Box 45 Kenora P9N 3X1 (807) 548-5100	40 km			X		X		X	Lodging nearby. Coffee shop, snack bar, lunch room.
Mount Madawaska Ltd. Box 632 Barry's Bay K0J 1B0 (613) 756-2931	15 km		X			X		X	Lodging nearby. Warming huts. Cookout shelter. Coffee shop, lunch room.
Neighick Resort Box 44 Ahmic Harbour P0A 1A0 (705) 387-3348	5 km		X			X		X	Sauna.
Nordic Nomad Ski Club Box 1416 Sioux Lookout P0V 2T0 (807) 737-2665	40 km		X			X		X	Lodging nearby. Coffee shop, lunch room.
Nordic Ski Club Box 648 Levack P0M 2C0 (705) 966-3917	45 km		X			X		X	Lodging nearby. Warming huts.

Name, Address and Telephone	Tracks		Gear Rentals		Instruction		Lodging		Other
	Groomed or Machine Set	Ungroomed	Yes	No	Yes	No	Yes	No	
Okimot Lodge Crystal Falls POH 1LO (705) 758-6719	20 km	50 km	X		X			X	
O-Pee-Chee Lake Lodge Marten River POH 1T0 (705) 892-2220	60 km		X		X			X	Warming huts. Lodge-to-lodge skiing.
Petawawa Crown Game Preserve Ski Trail Box 220 Pembroke K8A 6X4 (613) 732-3661	7 km		X		X			X	Lodging nearby.
Pine Top Ski Area RR 16 Thunder Bay P7B 6B3 (807) 683-8061	27 km		X		X			X	Lodging nearby. Snack bar. Warming huts.
Pinewood Park Motor Inn Box 687 North Bay P1B 8J8 (705) 472-0810 Toll Free: 1-800 461-9592	10 km		X		X			X	10 km lighted trail. Whirlpool, sauna.
Porcupine Ski Runners Box 250 Schumacher PON 1G0 (705) 235-8048	25 km		X		X		X		Snack bar, lunch room. Warming huts.

Name, Address and Telephone	Tracks Groomed or Machine Set	Ungroomed	Gear Rentals Yes	No	Instruction Yes	No	Lodging Yes	No	Other
Prince and Jarvis Ski Area Box 5000 Thunder Bay P7C 5G6 (807) 475-1531	36 km		X		X			X	
Ravenscroft Lodge RR 1 Temagami P0H 2H0 (705) 569-3865	120 km		X		X		X		Cookout shelter. Warming huts. Sauna. 2 km lighted trail.
Red Lodge Resort RR 1 Sheguiandah (Manitoulin Island) P0P 1W0 (705) 368-2388	10 km	30 km	X		X		X		Warming huts. Snowshoeing, snowmobiling, ice fishing.
Reeds Resort WB 84, RR 1, Reed's Road Whiskey Bay Hilton Beach (St. Joseph Island) P0R 1G0 (705) 246-2463	16 km		X		X		X		
Rendezvous Ski Club Box 25 Red Rock P0T 2P0 (807) 886-2421	12 km		X		X		X		Lodging nearby. Lunch room. Warming huts.

Name, Address and Telephone	Tracks Groomed or Machine Set	Ungroomed	Gear Rentals Yes	No	Instruction Yes	No	Lodging Yes	No	Other
Rene Brunelle Winter Recreation Area 6 Government Road Kapuskasing P5N 2W4 (705) 367-2442	11 km		X			X		X	Snack bar, lunch room. Warming huts.
Restoule Provincial Park Restoule P0H 2R0 (705) 729-2010	10 km			X		X		X	
Rockgarden Terrace Resort RR 1 Spring Bay P0P 2B0 (705) 377-4652	15 km		X			X		X	Whirlpool, sauna.
Rushing River Provincial Park Box 5080 Kenora P9N 3X9 (807) 468-9841	21 km			X		X		X	Lodging nearby. Cookout shelter.
Samuel de Champlain Provincial Park Box 147 Mattawa P0H 1V0 (705) 744-2276	20 km			X		X		X	Lodging nearby. Ice fishing, snowmobiling.
Sibley Provincial Park Box 5000 Thunder Bay P7C 5G6 (807) 475-1531	65 km			X		X		X	Lodging nearby.

Name, Address and Telephone	Tracks Groomed or Machine Set	Ungroomed	Gear Rentals Yes	No	Instruction Yes	No	Lodging Yes	No	Other
Sioux Narrows Provincial Park Box 5080 Kenora P9N 3X9 (807) 468-9841	5 km			X		X		X	Lodging nearby. Cookout shelter.
Stokely Creek Ski Touring Centre RR 1 Goulais River P0S 1E0 (705) 649-3421	100 km		X		X			X	Sauna. Warming huts. Transportation via Ontario Northland train.
Sunset Cove Lodge RR 2 Callander P0H 1H0 (705) 752-2820	15 km		X		X			X	Sauna.
Thorne Ski Resort RR 1 Thorne P0H 2J0 (819) 627-3529	20 km	50 km	X		X			X	Lodging nearby. Snack bar.
Tri-Town Ski Club Box 1598 New Liskeard P0J 1P0 (705) 672-3888	40 km		X		X		X		Snack bar, lunch room, cookout shelter.
Voima Athletic Club RR 4, Box 2, Site 35 Sudbury P3E 4M9 (705) 522-2890	40 km		X		X			X	Lodging nearby. Coffee shop.

Name, Address and Telephone	Tracks Groomed or Machine Set	Ungroomed	Gear Rentals Yes	No	Instruction Yes	No	Lodging Yes	No	Other
Walden Cross-Country Fitness Club Inc. Box 1198 Lively P0M 2E0 (705) 692-9557	9 km		X		X			X	Lodging nearby.
Walden Cross-Country Fitness Club Inc. Box 202 Naughton P0M 2M0 (705) 692-9557	8 km		X		X			X	Lodging nearby. Snack bar.
White Gables Box 21 Temagami P0H 2H0 (705) 237-8920	135 km		X		X			X	Cookout shelter.
Wildwaters Wilderness Skiing 119 Cumberland Street North Thunder Bay P7A 4M3 (807) 345-0111	20 km	unlimited	X		X			X	Warming huts, sauna. Ski guide, photo tours
Windsor Valley Ski Area 25 Algonquin Avenue Kirkland Lake P2N 1C1 (705) 567-7065	10 km		X		X			X	Warming huts.

Name, Address and Telephone	Tracks Groomed or Machine Set	Ungroomed	Gear Rentals Yes No	Instruction Yes No	Lodging Yes No	Other
Wishart Conservation Area Lakehead Region Conservation Authority Box 3476 Thunder Bay P7B 5J9 (807) 344-5857		9 km	X	X	X	

Southern Ontario

Name, Address and Telephone	Tracks Groomed or Machine Set	Ungroomed	Gear Rentals Yes	No	Instruction Yes	No	Lodging Yes	No	Other
Albion Hills Conservation Area Metro Toronto and Region Conservation Authority 5 Shoreham Drive Downsview M3N 1S4 (416) 661-6600	20 km		X		X			X	Lodging nearby. Skating, snowmobiling, snowshoeing. Coffee shop, snack bar.
Algonquin Nordic Ski Touring 65 Waterford Drive Townhouse 805 Weston M9R 2N7 Toronto (416) 248-6325	25 km	80 km	X		X			X	Warming huts. Whirlpool, sauna. Guided hut-to-hut wilderness tours.
Allandale Golf and Ski RR 4, Site 3 Barrie L4M 4S6 (705) 722-0404	15 km		X		X			X	Lodging nearby. Coffee shop.
Arrowhead Provincial Park RR 3 Huntsville P0A 1K0 (705) 789-5105	26 km			X	X			X	Lodging nearby. Cookout shelter. Warming huts. Skating, tobogganing.
Awenda Provincial Park Box 973 Penetanguishene L0K 1P0 (705) 549-2231	30 km	35 km		X	X			X	Lodging nearby. Cookout shelter. Warming huts.

Name, Address and Telephone	Tracks Groomed or Machine Set	Ungroomed	Gear Rentals Yes	No	Instruction Yes	No	Lodging Yes	No	Other
Bass Lake Provincial Park Box 2178 Orillia L3V 6S1 (705) 326-7054	5 km			X		X		X	Lodging nearby. Cookout shelter.
Bayview-Wildwood Resorts Port Stanton P0E 1L0 (705) 689-2338	16 km		X			X	X		Indoor pool, whirlpool, sauna, squash courts.
Bingeman Park 1208 Victoria Street North Kitchener N2B 3E2 (519) 744-1555	8 km		X		X			X	One lighted trail. Indoor roller skating, ice skating, tobogganing.
Birch Glen Resort Birch Glen Road Baysville P0B 1A0 (705) 767-3305	15 km		X		X		X		
Blue Mountain Resorts Ltd. RR 3 Collingwood L9Y 3Z2 (705) 445-0231		12 km	X		X		X		Dining room, snack bar. Daily bus from Toronto.
Bondi Village RR 1 Dwight P0A 1H0 (705) 635-2261	15 km		X		X			X	Cookout shelter huts.

Name, Address and Telephone	Tracks		Gear Rentals		Instruction		Lodging		Other
	Groomed or Machine Set	Ungroomed	Yes	No	Yes	No	Yes	No	
Bracebridge Resource Management Centre Box 1138 Bracebridge P0B 1C0 (705) 645-8747	16 km			X		X		X	Lodging nearby. Cookout shelter.
The Briars Inn Box 100 Jacksons Point L0E 1L0 (416) 722-3271 Toronto: (416) 364-5937	10 km			X	X		X		Warming huts. Indoor pool, whirlpool, sauna.
Bronte Creek Provincial Park 1219 Burloak Drive Burlington L7R 3X5 (416) 335-0023 Toronto: (416) 827-6911	11 km	25 km	X			X	X		Lodging nearby. Cookout shelter. Winter hiking, ice skating, tobogganing.
Bruce's Mill Conservation Area Metro Toronto and Region Conservation Authority 5 Shoreham Drive Downsview M3N 1S4 (Gormley) (416) 661-6600	12 km		X		X			X	Snack bar, lunch room.
Bud's Place* Kimberley N0C 1G0 (519) 599-5096	30 km		X		X		X		Lodging nearby.

Name, Address and Telephone	Tracks Groomed or Machine Set	Ungroomed	Gear Rentals Yes	Gear Rentals No	Instruction Yes	Instruction No	Lodging Yes	Lodging No	Other
Byrnell Golf and Ski Club Box 772 Fenelon Falls K0M 1N0 (705) 887-2935	38 km		X		X			X	Lodging nearby. Dining room, snack bar.
Camp Wawanaisa Box 42 Nobel P0G 1G0 (705) 342-9397	5 km		X		X			X	Indoor pool, whirlpool, sauna.
Cedar Grove Lodge Box 996 Huntsville P0A 1K0 (705) 789-4036	12 km		X		X			X	Whirlpool.
Cedar Mountain RR 7 Peterborough K9J 6X8 (705) 745-5251	21 km		X		X			X	Lodging nearby. Snack bar.
Christie Conservation Area Hamilton Region Conservation Authority Box 7099 Ancaster L9G 3L3 (416) 627-5116	9 km		X		X			X	Lodging nearby. Cookout shelter, snack bar. Skating, snowshoeing.
Chudleigh's Apple Farm Box 176 Milton L9T 4N9 (416) 878-2725 Toronto: (416) 270-2982	8 km	18 km	X		X			X	Lodging nearby. Coffee shop, snack bar. Sleigh and wagon rides

Name, Address and Telephone	Tracks Groomed or Machine Set	Ungroomed	Gear Rentals Yes No	Instruction Yes No	Lodging Yes No	Other
Cold Creek Conservation Area Metro Toronto and Region Conservation Authority 5 Shoreham Drive Downsview M3N 1S4 (416) 661-6600	11 km		X	X	X (No)	Snack bar, lunch room. Warming huts.
Cranberry Inn Box 37 Collingwood L9Y 3Z4 (705) 445-6600 Toronto: (416) 962-7925	10 km		X	X	X	Indoor pool.
Crane Lake House Rosseau Road P0C 1K0 (705) 378-2206	15 km		X	X	X	
Dagmar Resort Ltd. RR 1 Ashburn L0B 1A0 (416) 649-2002 Toronto: (416) 294-6385	15 km		X	X	X	Lodging nearby. Dining room, coffee shop.
Deerhurst Inn and Country Club Box 1950 Huntsville P0A 1K0 (705) 789-5543 Toronto: (416) 964-3925	25 km		X	X	X	1 km lighted trail. Indoor pool, whirlpool. Warming huts.

Name, Address and Telephone	Tracks Groomed or Machine Set	Ungroomed	Gear Rentals Yes	No	Instruction Yes	No	Lodging Yes	No	Other
Devil's Elbow Ski Resort Bethany L0A 1A0 (705) 277-2012	10 km		X		X			X	Dining room, coffee shop.
Divine Lake Lodge RR 1 Port Sydney P0B 1L0 (705) 385-2031	25 km		X		X		X		Snack bar, coffee shop, lunch room.
Dundas Valley Conservation Area Hamilton Region Conservation Authority Box 7099 Ancaster L9G 3L3 (416) 627-1233	36 km			X		X	X		Lodging nearby. Snack bar. Warming huts. Snowshoeing.
Earl Bales Park 5100 Yonge Street Willowdale M2N 5V7 (416) 638-5315	25 km		X		X		X		Lodging nearby. Snack bar.
Earl Rowe Provincial Park Box 966 Alliston L0M 1A0 (705) 435-4331	5 km			X		X	X		Lodging nearby. Cookout shelter.
Echo Hills Park RR 4, Huntsville Dwight P0A 1K0 (705) 635-1041	18 km		X			X	X		Warming huts.

Name, Address and Telephone	Tracks Groomed or Machine Set	Ungroomed	Gear Rentals Yes	Gear Rentals No	Instruction Yes	Instruction No	Lodging Yes	Lodging No	Other
Elmhirst's Four Seasons Resort RR 1 Keene K0L 2G0 (705) 295-4591	20 km		X			X		X	Indoor pool, whirlpool, sauna.
Elora Gorge Conservation Area Grand River Conservation Authority 400 Clyde Road Cambridge N1R 5W6	9 km		X			X		X	Lodging nearby. Winter camping by reservation. Snack bar.
Fares' Leisureland RR 2 Parry Sound P2A 2W8 (705) 378-2762	50 km			X		X		X	Lodging nearby.
Fern Resort RR 5 Orillia L3V 6H5 (705) 325-2256	12 km		X		X			X	Indoor pool, whirlpool, sauna.
Ferris Provincial Park Box 1409 Campbellford K0L 1L0 (613) 475-2204		9 km		X		X		X	Lodging nearby. Tobogganing.
Foxwood Inn RR 1 Dwight P0A 1H0 (705) 635-2333	10 km			X		X		X	

Name, Address and Telephone	Tracks Groomed or Machine Set	Ungroomed	Gear Rentals Yes No	Instruction Yes No	Lodging Yes No	Other
Ganaraska Forest Centre Ganaraska Region Conservation Authority Box 328 Port Hope L1A 3W4 (416) 797-2721	28 km		X	X	X	Lodging nearby. Snack bar, lunch room.
Georgian Nordic Ski Club Trail Box 42 Parry Sound P2A 2X2 (705) 746-2513	35 km		X	X	X	Lodging nearby. Dining room.
Goodrich-Loomis Conservation Area Lower Trent Region Conservation Authority 441 Front Street Trenton K8V 6C1 (613) 394-4829	15 km		X	X	X	Lodging nearby. Cookout shelter. Warming huts.
Grandview Farm Box 1089 Huntsville P0A 1K0 (705) 789-7462	10 km		X	X	X	
Gravenhurst KOA Nordic Trails RR 3 Gravenhurst P0C 1G0 (705) 687-2333	10 km		X	X	X	Lodging nearby. Lunch room, snack bar. Cookout shelter. Winter camping.

Name, Address and Telephone	Tracks Groomed or Machine Set	Ungroomed	Gear Rentals Yes	No	Instruction Yes	No	Lodging Yes	No	Other
Guindon Park Box 877 Collingwood K6H 5T9 (613) 932-4422	15 km			X		X		X	Lodging nearby.
Haliburton Forest Reserve Ltd. RR 1 Haliburton K0M 1S0 (705) 754-2198	40 km		X		X		X		Dining room, coffee shop.
Haliburton Highlands Cross-Country Ski Club Box 147 Minden K0M 2K0 (705) 286-1760	50 km		X		X			X	Lodging nearby. Cookout shelter.
Haliburton Lodge Box 269 Haliburton K0M 1S0 (705) 457-1556 Toronto: (416) 793-0566	10 km								Dining room. Whirlpool in suites, fireplace in cabins. Skating, snowshoeing, ice fishing, snowmobiling.
Harbour Inn and Resort Club Box 35 Brechin L0K 1B0 (705) 484-5365	10 km	9 km	X		X		X		
Harrison Park 75 2nd Avenue East Owen Sound N4K 2E5 (519) 376-0265	11 km		X		X			X	Lodging nearby. Coffee shop, snack bar.

Name, Address and Telephone	Tracks		Gear Rentals		Instruction		Lodging		Other
	Groomed or Machine Set	Ungroomed	Yes No		Yes No		Yes No		
Hart Lodge RR 2 Minden K0M 2K0 (705) 286-1738	6 km		X		X		X		
Harvest Village Box 22 Orangeville L9W 2Y8 (519) 941-8100	9 km		X		X		X		Sauna.
Heber Down Conservation Area Central Lake Ontario Conservation Authority 1650 Dundas Street E. Whitby L1N 2K8 (416) 579-0411	10 km		X		X		X		Lodging nearby. Cookout shelters. Snowshoeing.
Hidden Valley Highlands Ski Club Group Box 74 RR 4 Huntsville P0A 1K0 (705) 789-5942	7 km		X		X		X		Lodging nearby. Snack bar, lunch room.
Hilton Falls Conservation Area Halton Region Conservation Authority 310 Main Street Milton L9T 1P4 (416) 854-0262 Toronto: (416) 826-2855	10 km		X		X		X		Lodging nearby. Warming huts. Lunch room.

Name, Address and Telephone	Tracks Groomed or Machine Set	Ungroomed	Gear Rentals Yes	No	Instruction Yes	No	Lodging Yes	No	Other
Horseshoe Valley Resort Box 10 Barrie (705) 835-2790 Toronto: 1-800-461-0245	63 km		X		X		X		Whirlpool, sauna. Alpine skiing.
Inglis Falls Conservation Area North Grey Region Conservation Authority Box 759 Owen Sound N4K 5W9 (519) 376-3076	8 km	10 km	X		X		X		Lodging nearby.
Irwin Inn of Stoney Lake Inc. RR 2 Lakefield K0L 2H0 (705) 877-2240	116 km		X		X		X		
Kawartha Nordic Ski Club Trails* Box 1371 Peterborough K9J 7H6 (705) 742-1943	85 km		X		X		X		Lodging nearby.
Kawartha Peaks Ski Resort Inc. Box 472 Peterborough K9J 6Z6 (705) 277-2555		5 km	X		X		X		Lodging nearby. Snack bar.
Kerr Park Box 2079 Bracebridge P0B 1C0 (705) 645-9091	15 km		X		X			X	Cookout shelter.

Name, Address and Telephone	Tracks Groomed or Machine Set	Ungroomed	Gear Rentals Yes	No	Instruction Yes	No	Lodging Yes	No	Other
King's Forest Winter Park Box 150 Hamilton L8K 6M4 (416) 547-9042	10 km		X		X		X		Lodging nearby.
Lafontaine en Action RR 3 Penetanguishene L0K 1P0 (705) 533-2961	34 km		X		X		X		Lodging nearby. Warming huts. Cooking shelter.
L.M. Frost Natural Resources Centre Dorset P0A 1E0 (705) 766-2451	22 km		X		X		X		Lodging nearby. Cookout shelter. Warming hut.
Long Sault Conservation Area Central Lake Ontario Conservation Authority 1650 Dundas Street East Whitby L1N 2K8 (416) 579-0411		17 km	X		X			X	Snowshoeing.
Mansfield Outdoor Centre Mansfield L0N 1M0 (705) 435-4479	35 km		X		X		X		
Maple Brae Cottages Box 89 Emsdale P0A 1J0 (705) 636-5390	20 km		X		X		X		

Name, Address and Telephone	Tracks		Gear Rentals		Instruction		Lodging		Other
	Groomed or Machine Set	Ungroomed	Yes	No	Yes	No	Yes	No	
Maple Sands Resort RR 1 Haliburton K0M 1S0 (705) 754-2800 Toronto: (416) 281-3480	5 km		X			X	X		
Maple Trails RR 2 Millbrook L0A 1G0 (705) 932-2075	22 km		X		X			X	Snack bar, lunch room. Cookout shelter.
Metro Toronto Zoo Box 280 West Hill M1E 4R5 (416) 284-8181	10 km		X		X		X		Lodging nearby. Restaurant, snack bar. Metro zoo bus from Kennedy subway station.
The Millcroft Inn Box 889 Alton L0N 1A0 (519) 941-8111 Toronto: (416) 791-4422	10 km			X		X	X		Outdoor jacuzzi, whirlpool, sauna.
Molson Park* Big Bay Point Road S.S. no 1 Barrie L4M 4V3 (705) 726-6272 Toronto: (416) 361-1407	30 km		X		X		X		Lodging nearby. 25 km lighted trail. Coffee shop, snack bar.

Name, Address and Telephone	Tracks Groomed or Machine Set	Ungroomed	Gear Rentals Yes	No	Instruction Yes	No	Lodging Yes	No	Other
Moonstone Ski Resort Box 522 Coldwater L0K 1E0 (705) 835-2018 Toronto: (416) 368-6900	15 km		X		X			X	Coffee shop, snack bar.
Mosport Cross-Country Ski Park 73 Alness Street, Unit 6A Downsview M3J 2H2 (416) 665-6665	28 km		X		X				Warming huts. Coffee shop.
Mountain View Ski Hills* RR 2 Midland L4R 4K4 (705) 526-8149	13 km		X		X		X		Lodging nearby. Snack bar.
Mountsberg Wildlife Centre Halton Region Conservation Authority 310 Main Street Milton L9T 1P4 (416) 878-4131 Toronto: (416) 826-2855	13 km		X			X	X		Lodging nearby.
Mount St. Louis Ski Resort RR 4 Coldwater L0K 1E0 (705) 835-2112	16 km		X		X		X		Lodging nearby. Cafeteria.

Name, Address and Telephone	Tracks Groomed or Machine Set	Ungroomed	Gear Rentals Yes	No	Instruction Yes	No	Lodging Yes	No	Other
Muskoka Flag Inn RR 3 Utterson P0B 1M0 (705) 385-2624	10 km		X			X		X	Warming huts.
Muskoka Sands Inn RR 1 Gravenhurst P0C 1G0 (705) 687-2233	13 km		X			X		X	Indoor pool, whirlpool, sauna.
Nordic Inn Box 155 Dorset P0A 1E0 (705) 766-2343	20 km		X		X			X	2 lighted trails. Cookout shelter.
Nottawasaga Inn Box 1110 Alliston L0M 1A0 (705) 435-5501 Toronto: (416) 364-5068	12 km		X			X		X	Indoor pool, whirlpool, sauna.
Ox-Bow Lodge RR 4 Huntsville P0A 1K0 (705) 635-2514 Toll Free: 1-800-461-5815	25 km		X			X		X	

Name, Address and Telephone	Tracks Groomed or Machine Set	Ungroomed	Gear Rentals Yes	No	Instruction Yes	No	Lodging Yes	No	Other
Palgrave Forest and Wildlife Area Metro Toronto and Region Conservation Authority 5 Shoreham Drive Downsview M3N 1S4 (416) 661-6600	16 km		X		X			X	Lodging nearby.
Patterson Kaye Lodge RR 1 Bracebridge P0B 1C0 (705) 645-4169		5 km	X		X		X		
Pickerel Lake Lodge RR 2 Burks Falls P0A 1C0 (705) 382-2025	35 km		X		X		X		
Pine Lodge Resort Box 230 Port Sydney P0B 1L0 (705) 385-2271	20 km		X		X		X		
Pinehurst Lake Conservation Area Grand River Conservation Authority Box 729 Cambridge N1R 5W6 (519) 442-4721	9 km		X		X			X	Lodging nearby.

Name, Address and Telephone	Tracks Groomed or Machine Set	Ungroomed	Gear Rentals Yes	No	Instruction Yes	No	Lodging Yes	No	Other
Pinestone Inn and Country Club RR 2 Haliburton K0M 1S0 (705) 457-1800 Toronto: (416) 423-2000	35 km		X		X		X		Cookout shelter. Warming huts. Indoor pool, whirlpool, sauna.
Pleasure Valley Box 250 Claremont L0H 1E0 (416) 471-5070	20 km		X		X			X	Lodging nearby. Skating, sleigh rides. Snack bar, lunch room.
Port Sydney Ski Trail* Box 227 Port Sydney P0B 1L0 (705) 385-2327	20 km			X		X		X	Lodging nearby. Cookout shelter.
Pow-Wow Point Lodge Ltd. Box 387 Huntsville P0A 1K0 (705) 789-4951	15 km		X		X		X		Indoor pool, whirlpool, sauna.
Presqu'ile Provincial Park RR 4 Brighton K0K 1H0 (613) 475-2204	13 km		X		X			X	Lodging nearby. Winter camping.
Rankin Ski Trail Sauble Valley Conservation Authority Box 759 Owen Sound N4K 5W9 (519) 376-3076	12 km			X		X		X	Lodging nearby.

Name, Address and Telephone	Tracks Groomed or Machine Set	Ungroomed	Gear Rentals Yes	No	Instruction Yes	No	Lodging Yes	No	Other
Red Pine Motel Box 5 Alliston L0M 1A0 (705) 435-4381	24 km		X		X			X	Lighted outdoor skating.
Russ Haven Resorts Ltd. RR 2 Burks Falls P0A 1C0 (705) 382-2027	35 km		X		X			X	
Sandy Lane Resort RR 2 Minden K0M 2K0 (705) 489-2020 Toll Free: 1-800 461-1422	15 km		X		X			X	Whirlpool. Skating, snowmobiling, ice fishing.
Scanlon Creek Conservation Area South Lake Simcoe Conservation Authority Box 282 Newmarket L3Y 4X1 (416) 895-1281	6 km		X		X			X	Lodging nearby. Cookout shelter.
Seneca College RR 3 King City L0G 1K0 Toronto: (416) 833-3338	20 km		X		X			X	Lodging nearby. Snack bar, lunch room. Cookout shelter.

Name, Address and Telephone	Tracks Groomed or Machine Set	Ungroomed	Gear Rentals Yes	No	Instruction Yes	No	Lodging Yes	No	Other
Seymour Conservation Area Lower Trent Region Conservation Authority 441 Front Street Trenton K8V 6C1 (613) 394-4829	6 km			X		X		X	Lodging nearby. Cookout shelter.
Shamrock Lodge Box 218 Port Carling P0B 1J0 (705) 765-3177	23 km	40 km	X			X		X	Indoor pool, sauna
Shades Mills Conservation Area Grand River Conservation Authority 400 Clyde Road Cambridge N1R 5W6 (519) 621-3697	10 km		X			X		X	Lodging nearby. Snack bar.
Shanty Bay Golf and Nordic Country Club RR 2 Shanty Bay L0L 2L0 (705) 726-1922	27 km		X			X		X	Lodging nearby. Night skiing by appointment. Snack bar, lunch room.
Sheffield Greens Golf Club RR 3 Bobcaygeon K0M 1A0 (705) 738-2567	10 km		X			X		X	Lodging nearby. Cookout shelter. Coffee shop, snack bar.

Name, Address and Telephone	Tracks — Groomed or Machine Set	Tracks — Ungroomed	Gear Rentals — Yes	Gear Rentals — No	Instruction — Yes	Instruction — No	Lodging — Yes	Lodging — No	Other
Sherwood Inn Box 400 Port Carling P0B 1J0 (705) 765-3131	10 km			X		X	X		
Short Hills Provincial Park Reserve Box 1070 Fonthill L0S 1E0 (416) 892-2656	10 km			X		X		X	Lodging nearby.
Sibbald Point Provincial Park RR 2 Sutton West L0E 1R0 (416) 722-3268	8 km			X		X		X	Lodging nearby, camping. Cookout shelter. Skating, snowshoeing, ice fishing, snowmobiling.
Silent Lake Provincial Park RR 3, Cardiff Bancroft K0L 1C0 (613) 332-3940	44 km			X		X		X	Lodging nearby. Warming huts.
Sir Sams Inn Eagle Lake P.O. Haliburton K0M 1S0 (705) 754-2188 Toronto: (416) 283-2080	10 km		X			X	X		Whirlpool.
Ski Haven Resort RR 1 Gilford L0L 1R0 (705) 456-2026	22 km		X			X		X	Lodging nearby. Dining room, snack bar. Warming huts. Cookout shelter.

Name, Address and Telephone	Tracks Groomed or Machine Set	Ungroomed	Gear Rentals Yes	No	Instruction Yes	No	Lodging Yes	No	Other
Ski Medonte RR 11 Barrie L4M 4Y8 (705) 835-3010 Toronto: 1-800-461-0237	37 km		X		X			X	Lodging nearby. Cookout shelter. Coffee shop, lunch room.
Ski Woodnewton Ltd. RR 1 Claremont L0H 1E0 (416) 649-3044	15 km		X		X			X	Lodging nearby. Snack bar.
Snow Valley Ski Resort Box 46 Barrie L4M 4S9 (705) 728-9541	12 km		X		X			X	Lodging nearby. Cookout shelter. Coffee shop, lunch room.
Springwater Provincial Park Midhurst L0L 1X0 (705) 728-7393	11 km			X		X		X	Lodging nearby. Cookout shelter.
The Summit 10266 Yonge Street Richmond Hill L4C 4Y5 (416) 884-8621	20 km		X		X			X	Lodging nearby. Snack bar, lunch room.
Sunny Point Cottages Rosseau Road P0C 1K0 (705) 378-2505	12 km		X		X		X		Sauna, whirlpool. Warming huts.

Name, Address and Telephone	Tracks Groomed or Machine Set	Ungroomed	Gear Rentals Yes	No	Instruction Yes	No	Lodging Yes	No	Other
Sunny Rock Lodge RR 1 Minden K0M 2K0 (705) 286-2873	27 km		X			X			Cookout shelter. Warming huts.
Tally-Ho Inn Box 4500 Huntsville P0A 1K0 (705) 635-2281	20 km		X			X	X		Warming huts.
Terra Cotta Conservation Area Credit Valley Conservation Authority 10 Mill Street Meadowvale L0J 1K0 (416) 451-1615	11 km		X			X	X		Lodging nearby. Snack bar, lunch room.
The Townsend Trail Townsend Information Office 101 Nanticoke Creek Parkway Townsend N0A 1S0 (519) 587-2418 Toronto: (416) 585-7027	14 km		X			X		X	
Trillium Valley Ski Area Inc. 289 Porter Street Oshawa L1J 1N3 (416) 655-3754	30 km		X			X		X	3 km lighted trail. Snack bar, lunch room.

Name, Address and Telephone	Tracks — Groomed or Machine Set	Tracks — Ungroomed	Gear Rentals Yes	Gear Rentals No	Instruction Yes	Instruction No	Lodging Yes	Lodging No	Other
Tyrolean Village Resort RR 3, Box 9 Collingwood L9Y 3Z2 Toronto: (416) 921-0563		8 km	X		X		X		Sauna, indoor tennis courts.
Valens Conservation Area Hamilton Region Conservation Authority Box 7099 Ancaster L9G 3L3 (416) 659-7715	11 km		X		X			X	Lodging nearby. Skating, snowmobiling. Cookout shelter. Warming huts.
Vanderwater Conservation Area Moira River Conservation Authority 217 North Front Street Belleville K8P 3C3 (613) 968-3434	23 km				X			X	Cookout shelter.
Victoria County Forest Trail Ministry of Natural Resources Minden K0M 2K0 (705) 286-1521	9 km		X		X			X	Lodging nearby.
Wanapitei 7 Engleburn Place Peterborough K9H 1C4 (705) 743-3774		50 km	X	X	X		X		Sauna. Snowshoeing. Transportation by Lakeland Airways.

Name, Address and Telephone	Tracks Groomed or Machine Set	Ungroomed	Gear Rentals Yes	No	Instruction Yes	No	Lodging Yes	No	Other
Warsaw Caves Conservation Area Otonabee Region Conservation Authority 727 Lansdowne Street West Peterborough K9J 1Z2 (705) 745-5791	13 km			X		X		X	Cookout shelter.
Wasaga Beach Provincial Park Box 183 Wasaga Beach L0L 2P0 (705) 429-2516	21 km		X			X		X	Lodging nearby. Cookout shelter. Warming huts.
Whirlpool Golf Course Niagara Parks Box 150 Niagara Falls L2E 6T2 (416) 356-1140	12 km	10 km	X		X			X	Lodging nearby. Dining room, snack bar.
Whitefield Motor Hotel RR 2 Parry Sound P2A 2W8 (705) 378-2361	10 km		X		X		X		
Wig-A-Mog Inn RR 2 Haliburton K0M 1S0 (705) 457-2000	37 km		X		X		X		Cookout shelter. Indoor pool, whirlpool, sauna. Bus service from Toronto.

*Cross-country skiing events are held at these locations.

Eastern Ontario

Name, Address and Telephone	Tracks Groomed or Machine Set	Ungroomed	Gear Rentals Yes	No	Instruction Yes	No	Lodging Yes	No	Other
Baker's Valley RR 1 Arden K0H 1B0 (613) 478-2632	24 km		X		X			X	Cookout shelter. Snack bar.
Balahack Mountain Park RR 2 Tamworth K0K 3G0 (613) 379-2313	50 km		X		X			X	Coffee shop, snack bar. Cookout shelter. Warming huts.
Baxter Conservation Area Rideau Valley Conservation Authority Box 599 Manotick K0A 2N0 (613) 489-3592		5 km	X			X			Lunch room. Cookout shelter. Warming huts.
Black Ridge RR 5 Brockville KV6 5T5 (613) 345-1906	23 km		X		X		X		Lodging nearby. Cookout shelter. Snack bar.
Bon Echo Provincial Park RR 1 Cloyne K0H 1K0 (613) 336-2228 Toronto: (416) 965-3081	10 km		X		X		X		Lodging nearby.

Name, Address and Telephone	Tracks Groomed or Machine Set	Ungroomed	Gear Rentals Yes	No	Instruction Yes	No	Lodging Yes	No	Other
Brockville Rec Cross-Country Trail King Street East Brockville K6V 3P5 (613) 342-8772	7 km			X	X		X		Lodging nearby.
Browns Bay Park (St. Lawrence Parks) Box 740 Morrisburg K0C 1X0 (613) 543-2911	5 km		X		X			X	
Calabogie Peaks Box 13258 Kanata K2K 1X4 (613) 752-2720	16 km		X		X		X		Saturday tea dances.
Carillon Provincial Park Box 100 Chute-à-Blondeau K0B 1B0 (613) 674-2825	12 km		X		X			X	Cookout shelter.
Charleston Lake Provincial Park RR 4 Lansdowne K0E 1L0 (613) 659-2065 (416) 965-3081	16 km	20 km	X		X		X		Lodging nearby. Warming huts.
Club Boreal RR 1 Plantagenet K0B 1L0 (613) 673-5898	30 km		X		X		X		Coffee shop, snack bar.

Name, Address and Telephone	Tracks Groomed or Machine Set	Ungroomed	Gear Rentals Yes	No	Instruction Yes	No	Lodging Yes	No	Other
Craig Trails RR 2 Verona K0H 2W0 (613) 374-2248	15 km		X		X			X	Warming huts. Snack bar.
Crysler Farm Battlefield Park (St. Lawrence Parks) Box 740 Morrisburg K0C 1X0 (613) 543-2911	10 km		X		X			X	Snack bar.
Depot Lakes Conservation Area Napanee Region Conservation Authority 25 Ontario Street West Napanee K7R 3S6 (613) 354-3312	9 km		X		X		X		Lodging nearby. Cookout shelter.
Foley Mountain Conservation Area Rideau Valley Conservation Authority Box 599 Manotick K0A 2N0 (613) 273-3255	10 km		X		X		X		Lodging nearby. Lunch room. Warming huts.
Frontenac Provincial Park 1 Richmond Blvd. Napanee K7R 3S3 (613) 354-2173	10 km		X		X		X		

Name, Address and Telephone	Tracks Groomed or Machine Set	Ungroomed	Gear Rentals Yes	No	Instruction Yes	No	Lodging Yes	No	Other
Gould Lake Conservation Area Cataraqui Region Conservation Authority Box 160 Glenburnie K0H 1S0 (613) 546-4228	10 km			X		X		X	
Kemptville Nursery Forest RR 4 Kemptville K0G 1J0 (613) 258-3413	24 km			X		X		X	Lodging nearby.
Larose Forest Box 10 Bourget K0A 1E0 (613) 487-2100	18 km			X		X		X	Lodging nearby. Coffee shop, dining room.
Larose Forest Trails Box 308 Bourget K0A 1E0 (613) 487-2031	20 km			X		X		X	
Lemoine Point Conservation Area Cataraqui Region Conservation Authority Box 160 Glenburnie K0H 1S0 (613) 546-4228	5 km			X		X		X	Lodging nearby.

Name, Address and Telephone	Tracks Groomed or Machine Set	Ungroomed	Gear Rentals Yes	No	Instruction Yes	No	Lodging Yes	No	Other
Little Cataraqui Creek Conservation Area Cataraqui Region Conservation Authority Box 160 Glenburnie K0H 1S0 (613) 546-4228	6 km			X		X		X	Lodging nearby.
Macaulay Mountain Conservation Area Prince Edward Region Conservation Authority Box 310 Picton K0K 2T0 (613) 476-7408		11 km		X		X		X	Lodging nearby. Cookout shelter. Floodlit toboggan run.
Madawaska House RR 2 Palmer Rapids K0J 2E0 (613) 758-2396 Toronto: (416) 921-2557	14 km			X		X		X	Warming huts.
Maitland Trails Box 89 Maitland K0E 1P0 (613) 348-3625	36 km		X		X			X	Lodging nearby.
Mount Pakenham Box 190 Pakenham K0A 2X0 (613) 624-5290	35 km		X		X			X	Lodging nearby. 1 km lighted trail. Coffee shop. Cookout shelter. Warming huts.

Name, Address and Telephone	Tracks Groomed or Machine Set	Ungroomed	Gear Rentals Yes	No	Instruction Yes	No	Lodging Yes	No	Other
Murphys Point Provincial Park RR 5 Perth K7H 3C7 (613) 267-5060	12 km		X		X			X	Lodging nearby. Warming huts.
Nangor Lodge Box 3 Westmeath K0J 2L0 (613) 587-4455	36 km		X		X		X		
National Capital Commission Mer Bleue Trails 161 Laurier Avenue West Ottawa K1P 6J6 (613) 992-4231	19 km		X		X			X	Snack bar. Warming huts.
National Capital Commission Pine Grove Grails 161 Laurier Avenue West Ottawa K1P 6J6 (613) 992-4231	21 km		X		X			X	Lodging nearby.
National Capital Commission Forest Trails 161 Laurier Avenue West Ottawa K1P 6J6 (613) 992-4231	8 km		X		X			X	Lodging nearby.

Name, Address and Telephone	Tracks Groomed or Machine Set	Ungroomed	Gear Rentals Yes	No	Instruction Yes	No	Lodging Yes	No	Other
National Capital Commission Shirleys Bay Trails 161 Laurier Avenue West Ottawa K1P 6J6 (613) 992-4231	6 km	10 km		X		X		X	Lodging nearby.
National Capital Commission Stony Swamp Trails 161 Laurier Avenue West Ottawa K1P 6J6 (613) 992-4231	9 km	30 km		X		X		X	Lodging nearby.
Nordic Ski Club of Cornwall Box 1114 Cornwall K6J 2M3 (613) 932-5921	20 km		X		X		X		
Ottawa Rideau Trail Club Box 4616, Postal Station E Ottawa K1S 5H8		53 km		X		X		X	Lodging nearby. Warming huts. Trails extend from Kingston to Richmond Landing.
Palmerston Lake Sports Centre General Delivery Ompah K0H 2J0 (613) 479-2288	20 km			X		X		X	

Name, Address and Telephone	Tracks Groomed or Machine Set	Ungroomed	Gear Rentals Yes	No	Instruction Yes	No	Lodging Yes	No	Other
Sandbanks Provincial Park RR 1 Picton K0K 2T0 (613) 393-3314	12 km		X		X			X	Lodging nearby. Warming huts. Lunch room.
Shamokin Resort RR 2 Sharbot Lake K0H 2P0 (613) 335-5612		9 km	X		X			X	Transportation by bus from Toronto and Ottawa.
Stormont-Dundas and Glengarry County Forest 113 Amelia Street Cornwall K6H 5V7 (613) 933-1774	10 km		X		X			X	Lodging nearby.
The Triangle Cross Country Ski Club of Brockville Box 1277 Brockville K6V 5W2 (613) 342-7961	40 km		X		X			X	Cookout shelter. Warming huts.
Timbertown Trails Box 650 Renfrew K7V 4E7 (613) 432-6895	8 km		X		X			X	Snack bar. Warming huts. Horsedrawn sleigh rides, tobogganing.

Western Ontario

Name, Address and Telephone	Tracks: Groomed or Machine Set	Ungroomed	Gear Rentals: Yes	No	Instruction: Yes	No	Lodging: Yes	No	Other
Allan Park Management Unit Saugeen Valley Conservation Authority RR 1 Hanover N4N 3B8 (519) 364-1255	14 km			X		X		X	Lodging nearby.
A.W. Campbell Conservation Area St. Clair Regional Conservation Authority 205 Mill Pond Crescent Strathroy N7G 3P9 (519) 245-3710	5 km			X		X		X	Lodging nearby. Cookout shelter.
Backus Woods Long Point Regional Conservation Authority Box 525 Simcoe N3Y 4N5 (519) 426-4623	12 km			X		X		X	Lodging nearby. Rare example of Carolinian forest.
Bass Lake Lodge RR 1 Lombardy K0G 1L0 (613) 283-0136	15 km			X		X		X	
Benmiller Inn/Cherrydale Farm RR 4 Goderich N7A 3Y1 (519) 524-2191		11 km	X			X	X		Indoor pool, sauna, whirlpool.

Name, Address and Telephone	Tracks Groomed or Machine Set	Ungroomed	Gear Rentals Yes No	Instruction Yes No	Lodging Yes No	Other
Circle R Ranch Box 85 Delaware NOL 1E0 (519) 471-3799	18 km		X	X	X	Lodging nearby. 2 km lighted trail.
C.M. Wilson Conservation Area Lower Thames Valley Conservation Authority 100 Thames Street Chatham N7L 2Y8 (519) 354-7310		5 km	X	X	X	Lodging nearby. Cookout shelter.
Fanshawe Conservation Area Upper Thames River Conservation Authority Box 6278, Station D London N5W 5S1 (519) 451-2800	15 km		X	X	X	Lodging nearby. Snack bar, lunch room.
Greenhills RR 3 Lambeth NOL 1S0 (519) 652-5033	11 km		X	X	X	Lodging nearby. Dining room, snack bar. Warming huts. Sauna, indoor tennis.
Longwoods Road Conservation Area Lower Thames Valley Conservation Authority RR 1 Mount Brydges NOL 1W0 (519) 264-2420	6 km		X	X	X	Lodging nearby. Lunch room. Cookout shelter. Warming huts.

Name, Address and Telephone	Tracks Groomed or Machine Set	Ungroomed	Gear Rentals Yes	No	Instruction Yes	No	Lodging Yes	No	Other
Minto Glen Sports Centre Box 248 Harriston N0G 1Z0 (519) 338-5250	25 km		X		X		X		Lodging nearby. Snack bar. Cookout shelter.
Miramichi Leisure Time Park Box 1840 Port Elgin N0H 2C0 (519) 832-5918	15 km		X		X		X		Cookout shelter.
Morrison Dam Conservation Area Ausable Bayfield Conservation Authority Box 459 Exeter N0M 1S0 (519) 235-2610	6 km		X		X			X	
Naftel's Creek Conservation Area Maitland Valley Conservation Authority Box 5 Wroxeter N0G 2X0 (519) 335-3557		7 km	X		X		X		Lodging nearby.
Parkhill Conservation Area Ausable Bayfield Conservation Authority Box 459 Exeter N0M 1S0 (519) 235-2610	9 km		X		X			X	

Name, Address and Telephone	Tracks Groomed or Machine Set	Ungroomed	Gear Rentals Yes	No	Instruction Yes	No	Lodging Yes	No	Other
Pinery Provincial Park Box 490 Grand Bend N0M 1T0 (519) 243-3099	42 km		X			X		X	Lodging nearby. Snack bar, lunch room. Skating rink, toboggan hill.
Point Pelee National Park RR 1 Leamington N8H 3V4 (519) 326-3204	7 km		X			X		X	Lodging nearby. Snack bar. Cookout shelter.
Red Bay Lodge RR 1 Mar N0H 1X0 (519) 534-1027	40 km		X			X		X	Indoor pool, whirlpool, sauna.
Sauble Beach Cross-Country Ski Club Box F #5, RR 2 Hepworth N0H 1P0 (519) 371-2071	25 km		X			X		X	Lodging nearby.
Springwater Agreement Forest 353 Talbot Street West Aylmer West N5H 2S8 (519) 773-9241		7 km	X			X		X	Lodging nearby. Dining room, snack bar.
Springwater Conservation Area Catfish Creek Conservation Authority RR 5 Aylmer West N5H 2R4 (519) 773-9037		6 km	X			X	X		

Name, Address and Telephone	Tracks Groomed or Machine Set	Ungroomed	Gear Rentals Yes No	Instruction Yes No	Lodging Yes No	Other
Stoney Island Conservation Area Saugeen Valley Conservation Authority RR 1 Hanover N4N 3B8 (519) 364-1255	5 km		X (No)	X (No)	X (No)	Lodging nearby.
Summer House Park Miller Lake Road Miller Lake N0H 1Z0 (519) 795-7712	30 km		X (No)	X (No)	X (No)	Lodging nearby. Cookout shelter.
Sutton Park Inn Box 209 Kincardine N0G 2G0 (519) 396-3444	20 km		X (No)	X (No)	X (No)	Indoor pool, sauna.
The Little Inn of Bayfield Box 102 Bayfield N0M 1G0 (519) 565-2611		10 km	X (Yes)	X (Yes)	X (Yes)	
Victorian Inn 10 Romeo Street North Stratford N5A 5M7 (519) 271-4650	48 km	18 km	X (Yes)	X (Yes)	X (Yes)	Indoor pool, sauna.

Name, Address and Telephone	Tracks Groomed or Machine Set	Ungroomed	Gear Rentals Yes	No	Instruction Yes	No	Lodging Yes	No	Other
Wawanosh Valley Conservation Area Maitland Valley Conservation Authority Box 5 Wroxeter N0G 2X0 (519) 335-3557	10 km			X		X		X	Lodging nearby. Cookout shelter.
Wildwood Conservation Area Upper Thames River Conservation Authority Box 6278, Station D London N5W 5S1 (519) 284-2829	25 km			X		X		X	Lodging nearby. Snack bar, lunch room.

Manitoba

The number of ski clubs in Manitoba reflects the phenomenal growth of cross-country skiing in this province. Manitoba's ambitious Jackrabbit program, along with a dramatic increase in touring and racing events including an expanded masters program, indicate that the province is on the verge of greatness as far as cross-country skiing is concerned. In this province most skiing is done in the provincial parks, and the Manitoba Department of Natural Resources and local ski clubs should be contacted for necessary details.

For further information on cross-country skiing in Manitoba, contact:

Cross-Country Ski Association of Manitoba
1700 Ellice Avenue
Winnipeg, Manitoba R3H 0B1
(204) 788-5324
(204) 786-5641

Saskatchewan

With its fine network of seventeen provincial parks, and the many local golf courses operated by city parks and recreation departments, Saskatchewan offers the avid cross-country skier a wide and varied selection of cross-country trails.

Northern Saskatchewan will be of particular interest to wilderness skiers. There the majestic country of the Canadian Shield's western arm remains almost as it was when the early explorers and fur traders first reached it.

In the south the Cypress Hills rise suddenly above the surrounding ranchland to the height of 1,640 meters. The wooded slopes are the highest land between Labrador and the Rocky Mountains. Great ski conditions exist here.

As you ski the Cypress Hills, keep in mind the history of the place. Sitting Bull and his warriors escaped to this area from American retaliation after the Battle of the Little Big Horn in 1876. And underneath the snow of Cypress Hills Provincial Park lie the fossilized remains of sabretooth tigers, three-toed horses,

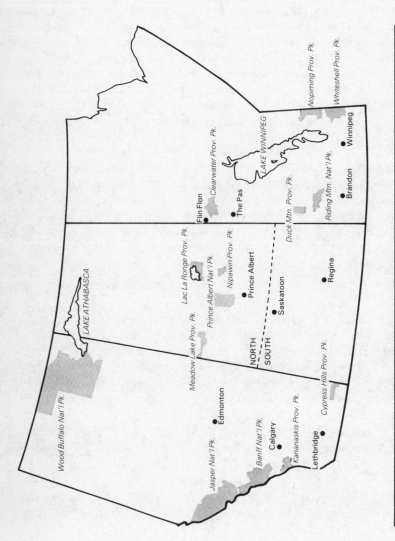

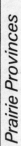

Prairie Provinces

and other amazing creatures millions of years old. (If this kind of natural history interests you, you can pay a visit to the nature center in the park while you're there, to view some of the local fossil finds.)

For more information about cross-country skiing in Saskatchewan, contact:

Linda Detta
1870 Lorne Street
Regina, Saskatchewan S4P 2L7
(306) 522-3651

Alberta

The rugged province of Alberta offers some marvellous possibilities for cross-country skiing. The cities of Edmonton and Calgary, in cooperation with their respective parks and recreation departments, have developed a fine network of cross-country trails. For the adventuresome skier the provincial parks of Alberta, nestled in the Canadian Rockies, offer an area of striking contrasts where snow-capped peaks loom over quiet valleys.

One such provincial park, Kananaskis, offers over seventy kilometers of cross-country trails. Most of the trails are designed to be "easy" or "intermediate" and contain few difficult sections.

North of Kananaskis Provincial Park on Highway 40 is the Ribbon Creek recreational area, offering forty kilometers of ski trails, and the Kananaskis Country Golf course with twelve kilometers of trails. Closer to Calgary at Bragg Creek, you'll find more than forty-five kilometers of ski trails of varying lengths and difficulty, and an additional thirty-seven kilometers at the Sandy McNabb reacreational area just west of Turner Valley.

Yet another popular cross-country retreat is the Alison-Chinook area, situated on gentle slopes below Mt. Tecumseh. There are eighteen kilometers of trails for beginners and intermediate cross-country skiers.

One unique service offered by the Alberta Provincial Parks and Recreation is the opportunity to arrange for an informal guided cross-country ski tour with an interpretive naturalist.

As extremely cold weather conditions can develop quickly

when skiing in such high mountain country as you find in Alberta, it is recommended that the following safety tips should be adhered to at all times:

1. Carry appropriate winter clothing, even on warm days.
2. Take along some extra woollen socks. They can make the difference between cold feet and frostbite. Woollen socks can be pulled over ski boots for increased insulation in case of an emergency or an extra cold day.
3. Take repair supplies—it can be a long, difficult walk if you break a ski! Carry cord, wire, pliers, knife, screwdriver, and an emergency ski tip.
4. High-energy foods (such as chocolate and/or dried fruit), waterproof matches and specially insulated blankets are invaluable in a winter emergency.
5. If you are caught in an avalanche, discard all equipment. Make swimming motions, try to stay on top, and work your way to the side of the avalanche. Do not cry out or open your mouth after you are in the avalanche. Get your hands in front of your face and try to make an air space as you are coming to a stop. If you are near the surface as the slide comes to a stop, thrust a hand or leg upward so that others can spot you.
6. Travel beyond designated areas is not recommended because of the danger of avalanches.
7. If you can plan to travel beyond designated areas or camp overnight, you may register your trip or obtain information at the Kananaskis Provincial Park Visitor Centre or the Barrier Lake Travel Information Centre.
8. Avoid skiing alone; ski with a companion.

For more information on cross-country skiing in Alberta, contact:

Cross-Country Alberta
14904-121A Avenue
Edmonton, Alberta T5V 1A3
(403) 452-4501

Calgary Ski Trails
City of Calgary Parks and Recreation
205–8th Avenue SE
Calgary, Alberta T2P 2M5
(403) 269-2531

Edmonton Ski Trails
City of Edmonton Parks and Recreation
10th floor, CN Tower
10004–104 Avenue
Edmonton, Alberta T5K 0K1
(403) 428-3559

Provincial Parks
Alberta Recreation and Parks
Standard Life Centre
10405 Jasper Avenue
Edmonton, Alberta T5N 3N4

Kananaskis Country
412–1001 Glenmore Trail SW
Calgary, Alberta T2V 4R6
(403) 297-3362

Manitoba

Name, Address and Telephone	Tracks Groomed or Machine Set	Ungroomed	Gear Rentals Yes	No	Instruction Yes	No	Lodging Yes	No	Other
Bakers Narrows Provincial Park 9 Terrace Street Flin Flon R8A 1S2 (204) 687-7834	36 km			X		X		X	Warming huts, chalet.
Birds Hill Provincial Park Box 183, RR2 Dugald ROE OKO (204) 222-9151	30 km		X			X		X	Warming huts. Restaurant.
Clearwater Provincial Park Box 2550 Third Street and Ross Avenue The Pas R9A 1M4 (204) 623-6411	16 km			X		X		X	Warming huts.
Duck Mountain Provincial Park Box 239 Swan River ROL 1Z0 (204) 734-2321	5 km			X		X		X	
Grand Beach Provincial Park Grand Beach ROE 0S0 (204) 754-2212	20 km			X		X		X	Warming huts.

Name, Address and Telephone	Tracks Groomed or Machine Set	Ungroomed	Gear Rentals Yes	No	Instruction Yes	No	Lodging Yes	No	Other
Hecla Provincial Park Box 70 Riverton ROC 2R0 (204) 378-2954	50 km		X		X			X	Warming huts. Lodge.
Riding Mountain National Park* Wasagaming ROJ 2H0 (204) 848-2811	200 km		X		X		X		Camping. Elkhorn Resort has sauna, whirlpool.
Sandilands Provincial Forest Box 2019 Steinbach ROA 2A0 (204) 326-4471	30 km		X		X			X	Warming huts.
Spruce Woods Provincial Park Box 900 Carberry ROK OHO (204) 834-3223	75 km		X		X		X		
Turtle Mountain Provincial Park Box 820 Boissevain ROK OEO (204) 534-2936	25 km		X		X			X	Warming huts.
Whiteshell Provincial Park Rennie ROE 1R0 (204) 369-5232	70 km		X		X			X	Manitoba Wilderness Centre has lodging, sauna.

*Cross-country skiing events are held at these locations.

Northern Saskatchewan

Name, Address and Telephone	Tracks Groomed or Machine Set	Ungroomed	Gear Rentals Yes	No	Instruction Yes	No	Lodging Yes	No	Other
Bainbridge Lodge 88 km north of Hudson Bay at jct. Hwy 9 and 55 Phone Mobile Radio Operator at The Pas YJ6-3654	55 km			X		X		X	
Battlefords Provincial Park 40 km north of North Battleford via Hwy 4 (306) 386-2313	42 km			X		X		X	Lodging nearby. Ice fishing, snowshoeing.
Candle Lake Minowukaw Beach and Bay Lake Areas (306) 929-4656	21 km			X		X		X	Rentals at Snow Castle lodge.
Carrot River 6.4 km east and 3.2 km north of Carrot River (306) 768-3833	2.8 km		X		X			X	
Christopher Lake Lutheran Cross-Country Adjacent to Lutheran Church Camp, 35 km north of Prince Albert, 7 km northwest via Hwy 263 (306) 982-4758	3 km		X		X			X	

Name, Address and Telephone	Tracks Groomed or Machine Set	Ungroomed	Gear Rentals Yes	No	Instruction Yes	No	Lodging Yes	No	Other
Cooke Municipal Golf Course 22nd St. and 10th Avenue West Prince Albert	8 km			X		X		X	Gear rentals in Prince Albert. Lodging nearby.
Cudworth Ski Trails South on 6th Avenue in Cudworth Contact John Diedericks (306) 256-7075	13 km		X		X			X	Lighted downhill-ski tow.
Denare Beach Amishi Trails Denare Beach, 16 km southwest of Flin Flon on Hwy 167 (306) 362-2232	4 km			X		X		X	Gear rentals available in Flin Flon.
Emma Lake/Oscar Lake Adjacent to Birch Bay II Cottage Development on Emma Lake (306) 982-2002		39 km		X		X		X	New area under development. Lodging nearby. Snowmobiling.
Fort A La Corne Provincial Forest Covers two areas Gronlid Trails, 10 km north of Gronlid and west Lars Trails, 25 km north of Kinistino (306) 752-4793		17 km		X		X		X	Lodging nearby.

Name, Address and Telephone	Tracks Groomed or Machine Set	Ungroomed	Gear Rentals Yes	No	Instruction Yes	No	Lodging Yes	No	Other
Greenwater Provincial Park 30 km southwest of Porcupine Plain and 48 km north of Kelvington on Hwy 38 (306) 278-2972	26 km			X		X		X	Gear rental available at Weigh Anchor Marina 278-3200. Ice fishing, snowshoeing, skating.
Hudson Bay Regional Park 2 km south of Hudson Bay (Town) (306) 865-3712	5 km			X		X		X	Lodging nearby.
Jacobsen Bay Outfitters Anglin Lake 60 km north of Prince Albert, 8 km west of Hwy 2 (306) 663-5844		37 km	X			X		X	Sauna. Seven provincially operated trails.
Kipabiskau Regional Park 32 km south of Tisdale via Hwy 35, 9.6 km west on Grid Road (306) 873-4914	6 km			X		X		X	Lodging nearby. Ice fishing, skating, tobogganing, snowshoeing, snowmobiling.
Lac La Ronge Provincial Park* Skiing areas include English Bay and Nut Point (306) 425-3737	75 km		X		X			X	Lodging nearby. Gear rentals at Kiginak ski rental.

Name, Address and Telephone	Tracks Groomed or Machine Set	Ungroomed	Gear Rentals Yes	No	Instruction Yes	No	Lodging Yes	No	Other
Little Bear Lake Resort Mile 62 Hanson Lake Road via Prince Albert Phone Mobile Operator JR3-2049 Narrow Lake Tower	40 km			X	X			X	Torchlight skiing on New Year's Eve.
Little Red River Park 3 km east of Prince Albert via Hwy 55 (306) 922-9643	50 km		X		X			X	Lodging nearby.
McPhee Lake Cabin McPhee Lake Hwy 264 near entrance to Prince Albert National Park (306) 663-5361		10 km	X			X		X	Snowmobiling.
Meadowlake Nordic Ski Club* In St. Cyr Hills, 14 km east of Meadow Lake on Hwy 55, 1.5 km north on Island Hill Road (306) 236-4182 or 236-5777	130 km		X		X			X	Lodging nearby. Gear rentals available at J & E Sporting Goods.
Meadow Lake Provincial Park 6.4 km north of Dorintosh via Hwy 4, approximately 39 km north of Meadow Lake (306) 236-3382	30 km			X	X			X	Lodging nearby.
Nipawin Provincial Park Lower Fishing Lake at Mile 46. Hanson Lake Road via Hwys 55 and 106 from Prince Albert (306) 426-2082	18 km		X			X		X	Gear rentals available in Prince Albert. Snowmobiling, ice fishing.

Name, Address and Telephone	Tracks Groomed or Machine Set	Ungroomed	Gear Rentals Yes	No	Instruction Yes	No	Lodging Yes	No	Other
Nisbet Campground 1 km north of Prince Albert via Hwy 2	4 km		X			X		X	Lodging nearby. Gear rentals available in Prince Albert. Trails lighted for night use.
Prince Albert National Park 88 km north of Prince Albert via Hwys 2 and 264 (306) 633-5322		89 km	X			X		X	Gear rentals at McPhee and Anglin Lakes. Ice fishing at Waskesiu Lake only. Wilderness skiing, snowshoeing.
Shell River Located at Shell River Campground 14 km west of Prince Albert, south side of Hwy 3 (306) 922-9897	8 km			X		X		X	Lodging nearby. Snowmobiling.
Ships' Lantern Hotel Hwy 120, north of Meath Park on Candle Lake (306) 929-4555	Trails nearby, see other Candle Lake listings			X		X		X	Ice fishing, skating.
Snow Castle Lodge On Torch Lake in the Candle Lake area Hwy 120 (306) 929-2174 or 989-4403	30 km			X		X		X	Gear rentals available in Prince Albert. Snowmobiling, indoor pool, snowshoeing.

Name, Address and Telephone	Tracks Groomed or Machine Set	Ungroomed	Gear Rentals Yes	No	Instruction Yes	No	Lodging Yes	No	Other
Stabler Point 5 km west of Loon Lake in Makiva Lake Recreation Site, at Stabler Point (306) 837-2092	18 km			X		X		X	Lodging nearby.
Wapiti Valley Regional Park 14.5 km north of Gronlid via Hwy 6 (306) 428-2822	5 km		X			X		X	Lodging nearby.
Watson's Resort Lac la Plonge (306) 288-2122		unlimited	X			X		X	Snowmobiling, ice fishing.
Whiteswan Lodge* Located on Whiteswan Lake, approx. 110 km northeast of Prince Albert via Hwys 55 and 120 and Gravel Road Phone Mobile Telephone JR3-2048 registered at Narrow Lakes		10 km	X					X	Gear rentals available in Prince Albert. Snowmobiling.

*Cross-country skiing events are held at these locations.

Southern Saskatchewan

Name, Address and Telephone	Tracks Groomed or Machine Set	Ungroomed	Gear Rentals Yes	No	Instruction Yes	No	Lodging Yes	No	Other
Beaver Creek Conservation Area 16 km south of Saskatoon on Larne Avenue (306) 665-6887		km not stated		X		X		X	Lodging nearby.
Blackstrap Lake Recreation Site 32 km south of Saskatoon via Hwy 11 and 8 km east of Dundurn (306) 492-2276	5 km			X		X		X	Lodging nearby. Skating, tobogganing, ice fishing.
Buffalo Pound Provincial Park 27 km northeast of Moose Jaw, via Hwy 2, 202 & 301 (306) 694-3659 or 693-1333	5 km		X			X		X	Lodging nearby. Skating, tobogganing, ice fishing, snowshoeing.
Carlton Trail Regional Park 40 km south of Langenburg via Hwy 8, 8 km south of Spy Hill (306) 743-2971	6.4 km		X		X			X	Lodging nearby.
Carlton Trail Ski Club From Humbolt 6.5 km west via Hwy 5, 6.5 km north on Grid Road & 3.2 km west (306) 682-5557	17 km			X		X		X	Lodging nearby. Gear rentals in Saskatoon.
Cranberry Flats 13 km south of Saskatoon (306) 665-6887		km not stated	X			X		X	Lodging nearby.

Name, Address and Telephone	Tracks		Gear Rentals		Instruction		Lodging		Other
	Groomed or Machine Set	Ungroomed	Yes	No	Yes	No	Yes	No	
Crystal Beach Regional Park 2.4 km southwest of Harris via Hwy 7 (306) 656-2134		X		X		X		X	Lodging nearby. Gear rentals available in Saskatoon.
Cypress Hills Provincial Park 27 km south of Maple Creek via Hwy 21 (306) 662-4411	21 km		X			X		X	Indoor hot tub, sauna. Downhill skiing, snowmobiling, skating, ice fishing.
Deer Park Golf Course Located at junction Hwys 10 and 52 at Yorkton (306) 783-5622	19 km			X		X		X	Lodging nearby. Trails lighted for night use. Tobogganing.
Duck Lake Area Eb's Trails Nisbet Provincial Forest, 8 km north of Duck Lake via Hwy 11 (306) 652-0385		32 km	X			X		X	Gear rentals available in Saskatoon.
Duck Mountain Provincial Park 21 km east of Kamsack via Hwys 5 and 57 (306) 542-3482	65 km			X		X		X	Tobogganing, skating, snowshoeing, ice fishing.
Duck Mountain Regional Park* Located at Bogg Creek, 21 km east of Kamsack via Hwy 5 (306) 542-4111	32 km			X		X		X	Lodging nearby.

Name, Address and Telephone	Tracks Groomed or Machine Set	Ungroomed	Gear Rentals Yes	No	Instruction Yes	No	Lodging Yes	No	Other
Echo Valley Provincial Park 8 km west of Fort Qu'Appelle via Hwy 210 (306) 332-5615	10 km			X		X		X	Lodging nearby. Ice fishing, snowshoeing.
Forestry Farm Park Northeast of Sutherland, north of 115th Street Saskatoon	12 km			X		X		X	Lodging nearby. Concession open weekends.
Good Spirit Lake Provincial Park 50 km northwest of Yorkton via Hwys 9 and 229 (306) 782-2006	15 km			X		X		X	Lodging nearby. Gear rentals in Yorkton.
Grassick Park/Les Sherman Park Operated by City of Regina Parks and Recreation (306) 569-7392	9 km			X		X		X	Lodging nearby. Gear rentals available in Regina.
Holiday Park Golf Course Operated by City of Saskatoon Parks and Recreation Department Located on Avenue "U" southwest of Saskatoon (306) 664-9340	6 km			X		X		X	Lodging nearby. Gear rentals and instruction available in Saskatoon.
Kinookimaw Beach Golf & Country Club 48 km north of Regina via Hwys 11 and 54 (306) 729-2295	3 km			X		X		X	Gear rentals available in Regina.

Name, Address and Telephone	Tracks Groomed or Machine Set	Ungroomed	Gear Rentals Yes	No	Instruction Yes	No	Lodging Yes	No	Other
Kinsmen Park Operated by City of Saskatoon Parks and Recreation Department (306) 664-9340	1.5 km		X		X		X		Lodging nearby. Gear rentals and instruction available in Saskatoon.
Lloydminster Cross-Country Ski Club 15 km east, 5 km north of Lloydminster (306) 825-7632	Numerous tracks		X		X		X		Lodging nearby.
Melville Regional Park* Northeast side of Melville off Hwy 10 (306) 728-4545	10 km			X		X	X		Lodging nearby.
Moose Jaw River Park Contact 693-3621 ext. 35 for information	14 km			X		X	X		Lodging nearby.
Moose Mountain Provincial Park 58 km south of Whitewood	48 km		X			X	X		Lodging nearby. Gear rentals at Kenosee Gardens. Skating, ice fishing, snowshoeing.
Murray Golf Course/Kings Park Operated by City of Regina Parks and Recreation Department, located 11 km northeast of Regina (306) 569-7392	22.5 km		X		X		X		Lodging nearby. Tobogganing.

Name, Address and Telephone	Tracks		Gear Rentals		Instruction		Lodging		Other
	Groomed or Machine Set	Ungroomed	Yes	No	Yes	No	Yes	No	
Ochapowace Band Ski Resort (Formerly Last Oak Park) 3 km east of Broadview on Hwy 1, then 18 km north on Hwy 201	7 km			X		X		X	Lodging nearby.
River Bank Operated by City of Saskatoon Parks and Recreation Department, located on north side of river (306) 664-9340		20 km	X			X		X	Lodging nearby. Gear rentals and instruction available in Saskatoon.
Rowan's Ravine Provincial Park 90 km northwest of Regina via Hwys 11, 20, and 220 (306) 725-4423		1.5 km						X	Lodging nearby. Skating, ice fishing.
Saskatchewan Landing Provincial Park 70 km north of Swift Current (306) 773-1521	6 km		X			X		X	Lodging nearby. Snowmobiling.
Sea Surf Inn Manitou Beach Box 404 Watrous S0K 4T0 (306) 946-2110	Various trails		X			X		X	Tobogganing.
Sturges-Assiniboine Ski Area 3 km south of Sturges (306) 548-2852 or 548-2966		2 km	X			X		X	Lodging nearby.

Name, Address and Telephone	Tracks Groomed or Machine Set	Tracks Ungroomed	Gear Rentals Yes	Gear Rentals No	Instruction Yes	Instruction No	Lodging Yes	Lodging No	Other
Wascana Centre* Located in South Regina (306) 522-3661	10 km			X		X		X	Lodging nearby. Some trails lighted for night use.
West River Bank Starts at Bessborough Hotel, extending to Meewasin Park, Saskatoon	4.5 km			X		X		X	Lodging nearby. Gear rentals and instruction available in Saskatoon.
Weyburn Cross-Country Ski Trail Northwest of Weyburn junction via Hwys 35 and 13 (306) 842-4911	18 km			X		X		X	Lodging and gear rentals available.
White Butte Located 4 km north of White City on Grid Road west of junction Hwys 1 and 48		11 km plus		X		X		X	Lodging nearby.
Wildwood Golf Course Operated by City of Saskatoon Parks and Recreation Department (306) 664-9340	4 km		X		X			X	Lodging, gear rentals and instruction available in Saskatoon.
York Lake Regional Park 5 km south of Yorkton	11 km			X		X		X	Lodging and gear rentals available in Yorkton.

*Cross-country skiing events are held at these locations.

Alberta

Name, Address and Telephone	Tracks Groomed or Machine Set	Ungroomed	Gear Rentals Yes	No	Instruction Yes	No	Lodging Yes	No	Other
A and H Dude Ranch RR 1 Elnora T0M 0Y0 (403) 773-2442	10 km		X				X		Sleigh rides.
Alberta Wildlife Park RR 1 Legal T0G 1L0 (403) 921-3918	4 km								
Al Oemings Polar Park 51419 Range Road, #223 Sherwood Park T8C 1H4 (403) 922-3013	10 km								Sleigh rides, ski trails, Surrounding game enclosure. (Cold-climate animal wildlife park).
Banff Alpine Guides Box 1025 Banff T0L 0C0 (403) 678-5468		unlimited			X		X		Lodging, camping. Telemarking. Avalanche courses.
Black Cat Guest Ranch Box 542, Hinton T0E 1B0 (403) 866-2107	70 km						X		Guided tours.

Name, Address and Telephone	Tracks		Gear Rentals		Instruction		Lodging		Other
	Groomed or Machine Set	Ungroomed	Yes	No	Yes	No	Yes	No	
Camp Apa Cheesta Box 803 Hinton TOE 1BO (403) 865-7877		unlimited	X			X	X		Lodging, winter camps. Willmore Wilderness & Jasper National Park, also dog sledding.
Clarey Bush Outfitting and Guiding Jasper National Park Box 84 Jasper TOE 1EO (403) 852-3078		unlimited					X		Lodging A-tents, Cabins. Dog sledding. Overnight excursions for cross-country skiers. Snowshoeing.
Haus Alpenrose Tourist Rooms, Bed and Breakfast Home of the Canadian School of Mountaineering Box 723 Canmore TOL OMO		unlimited	X			X	X		Avalanche course, waterfall ice climbing, glacier touring.
Hidden Ridge* Located in Strathcona Provincial Science Park (403) 471-3642			X			X		X	Skating, tobogganing, downhill skiing.
Homeplace Ranch RR 1 Priddis TOL 1NO (403) 931-3245		marked trails					X		Near Bragg Creek. Sleigh rides.

Name, Address and Telephone	Tracks Groomed or Machine Set	Ungroomed	Gear Rentals Yes	No	Instruction Yes	No	Lodging Yes	No	Other
Jasper Climbing School Box 452 Jasper TOE 1EO (403) 852-3964		unlimited						X	Avalanche course. Ice climbing courses. Mountaineering school. 3 & 4 day ski touring.
Jasper Wilderness and Tonquin Valley Ski Trips Box 550 Jasper TOE 1EO (403) 852-3909		unlimited						X	Guided tours.
Lac Des Arcs Climbing School c/o 1116-19 Avenue N.W. Calgary T2M 0Z9 (403) 289-6795		unlimited	X		X			X	Mountaineering. Snow and ice climbing.
Mistaki Super Wilderness Tours Box 90 Fort Chipewyan TOP 1BO (403) 697-3693		50 km						X	Lodging in tents, tipis or lodge. Ice fishing, dog sledding, hot tub, sauna, snowshoeing.
Skoki Lodge Box 5 Lake Louise TOL 1EO (403) 522-3555	35 km		X		X			X	Guided tours. Telemarking.

Name, Address and Telephone	Tracks Groomed or Machine Set	Ungroomed	Gear Rentals Yes	No	Instruction Yes	No	Lodging Yes	No	Other
Spruce Valley 15 km east of Fort McMurray on Airport Road (403) 743-0796			X			X		X	Downhill skiing.
Sunshine Village* Box 1510 Banff TOL 0C0 (403) 762-3383	20 km		X			X		X	Downhill skiing. Jacuzzi, sauna. Guides available.
Terratima Cross-Country Ski Hostel Box 1636 Rocky Mountain House TOM 1T0 (403) 845-6786	75 km		X			X		X	Night skiing. Wood-fired sauna.
Woodlea Ski Hill 55th St. and 42nd Avenue Red Deer (403) 342-8260			X					X	Tobogganing, skating.

*Cross-country skiing events are held at these locations.

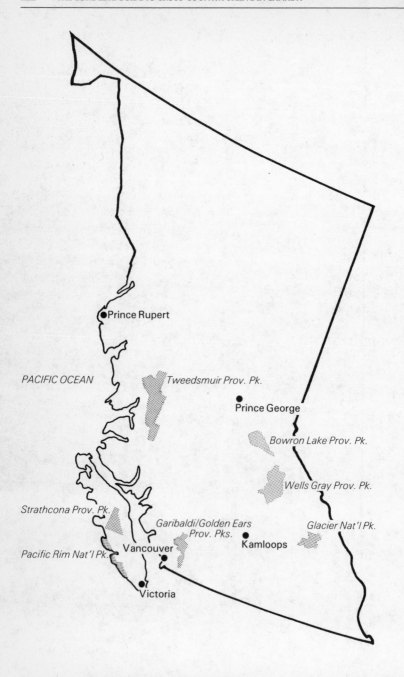

PACIFIC OCEAN

●Prince Rupert

Tweedsmuir Prov. Pk.

●
Prince George

Bowron Lake Prov. Pk.

Wells Gray Prov. Pk.

Strathcona Prov. Pk.

Garibaldi/Golden Ears
Prov. Pks.

Glacier Nat'l Pk.

Pacific Rim Nat'l Pk.

Vancouver

●
Kamloops

●
Victoria

British Columbia

British Columbia

Four major ski resorts and endless cross-country terrain are presided over by the magnificent Rocky Mountains in British Columbia from the Trans-Canada Highway to the United States border. All four resorts—Panorama, Fairmont, Kimberly, and Fernie Snow Valley—offer on-hill accommodation for all tastes and preferences. Fairmont Hot Springs even offers a unique package that includes hot mineral pools and free skiing for persons eight years of age and under or sixty years of age and over.

The Okanagan/Kamloops area boasts ample snow and moderate temperatures. One of the outstanding cross-country ski centers in this area is the Lac le Jeune Resort located just southwest of Kamloops. Lac le Jeune offers an extensive network of trails for the recreational skier along with family accommodation.

For more information on cross-country skiing in British Columbia, contact:
Billie Bartley
1200 Hornby Street
Vancouver, British Columbia V6Z 2E2
(604) 687-3333, ext. 54

British Columbia

Name, Address and Telephone	Tracks Groomed or Machine Set	Ungroomed	Gear Rentals Yes	No	Instruction Yes	No	Lodging Yes	No	Other
Big White Box 2039, Station R Kelowna V1X 4K5 1-800 633-4204	25 km								
Cypress Cross-Country Area 1600 Indian River Drive North Vancouver V7G 1L3 (604) 929-8171	30 km		X		X		X		Lodging nearby. Alpine skiing, snowshoeing, tobogganing.
Fairmont Hot Springs Resort Box 10 Fairmont Hot Springs V0B 1L0 (604) 345-6311	20 km						X		
Fernie Snow Valley Box 788 Fernie V0B 1M0 (604) 423-9221	6 km	20 km					X		
Harper Mountain 2042 Valleyview Drive Kamloops V2C 4C5 (604) 573-5115	15 km								

Name, Address and Telephone	Tracks		Gear Rentals		Instruction		Lodging		Other
	Groomed or Machine Set	Ungroomed	Yes	No	Yes	No	Yes	No	
Panorama Resort Box 7000 Invermere V0A 1K0 (403) 260-9400 (604) 342-6941	20 km						X		
Ptarmigan Tours Unlimited 160 Higgins Street Kimberly V1A 1K6 (604) 427-4029		unlimited	X		X		X		Avalanche seminar. Telemarking.
Radium/Edgewater Trail System c/o The Sports Chalet Box 10 Radium Hot Springs V0A 1M0 (604) 347-9591	15 km						X		Lodging nearby.
Red Mountain Ski Area Box 939 Rossland V0G 1Y0 (604) 362-7384	15 km	50 km	X		X		X		Lodging nearby.
108 Mile Ranch Resort* Compartment 2, RR 1 100 Mile House V0K 2E0 (604) 791-5211	100 km		X		X		X		Whirlpool, sauna. Sleigh rides, ice skating.

*Cross-country skiing events are held at these locations.

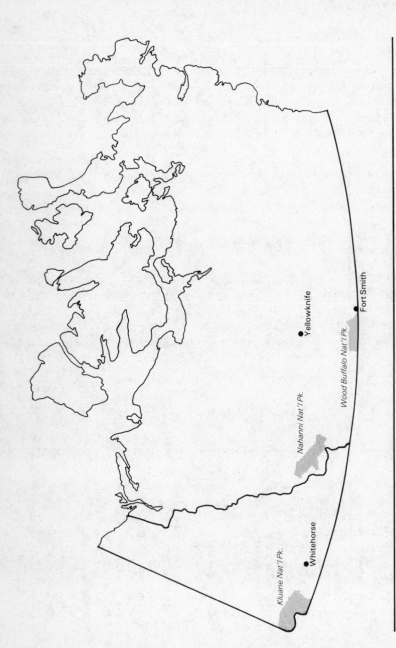

Yukon and Northwest Territories

Northwest Territories

Make no mistake; you would indeed have to be a very intrepid soul—as well as a very good skier—to pursue a ski "holiday" in the Northwest Territories. Inaccessibility, isolation, and extreme conditions are the major obstacles, but if you are up to the challenge (and the expense), follow up on the Subarctic Wilderness Adventure. If you do so, I guarantee that the ski stories you bring back with you will fill your skiing acquaintances with absolute awe.

Cross-country skiing in the Northwest Territories can be arranged through:
Subarctic Wilderness Adventures
Box 685
Fort Smith, NWT X0E 0P0
(403) 872-2467

Skiing tours are arranged with dogsled (either "you-drive" or with "in-sled" support), ski touring, and/or snowshoeing. Accommodation may be hut-to-hut, family-to-hut, tent, or tipi. Pension accommodation is available for the first and last nights of the tour. A full range of clothing, equipment, and sleds can be rented. Access to Fort Smith and Fort Chipewyan is by bush road or by Pacific Western Airlines.

Yukon

The Yukon is one of the world's last frontiers. All of the Yukon except for a small strip in the north is actually a subarctic region, and the weather is not nearly as harsh as most people suppose. Winter temperatures on average are about the same as in Winnipeg and Saskatoon. Snowfall is not heavy as the Yukon only receives approximately 150 centimeters per year in the northern regions, but the Whitehorse cross-country ski club members can be relied on to point you in the right direction for excellent skiing.

Kluane National Park in southwestern Yukon, a 25,600-square-kilometer wilderness sanctuary, may be suggested as ideal for wilderness skiers. A "must visit" if you're in the Yukon, especially if you're good with a camera, Kluane's mountains include Mount Logan, Canada's highest peak at 6,050 meters.

Cross-country skiing in the Yukon may be arranged through:
Whitehorse Cross-Country Ski Club
Whitehorse, Yukon
(403) 668-4344

Equipment rentals, instructions, and lodging can all be arranged. There are ninety kilometers of ungroomed tracks. The club features night skiing.

Appendices

The Latest in Touring and Light Touring Skis • Racing Skis

Appendix One

The Latest in Touring and Light Touring Skis

THE LATEST IN TOURING AND LIGHT TOURING SKIS

Manufacturer	Brand Name	Dimension	Wax or Waxless	Core	Performance Observations	Other Observations
Atomic	Microstep 15	48 mm Parallel Cut	Waxless			In-track ski with microstep base
Edsbyn	MT252	53/50/52 mm	Waxless			Designed for in-off track all-around use
Elan	Elan FW 240	53/50/52 mm	Wax	Wood Core		Versatile; in-track and off-track
Elan	Elan FW 241	53/50/52 mm	Waxless	Wood Core		
Haga	Haga 502	52/48/50 mm	Wax			Offers just enough sidecut for off-track but not enough to interfere with in-track touring
Hagan	Tri Steps	45 mm Parallel Cut	Wax		Fast and lively in-track performers	P-Tex racing type base
Jarvinen	Laser 46	46 mm Parallel Cut	One set of fibers set at 45° angles, second set of stubby fibers set at lower angles			Manufacturer claims that grip is effective for temperatures around freezing and for colder, powder snow conditions
Jarvinen	Lynx G & G	51/48/50 mm Sidecut	Waxless		Used mainly for in-track	G & G stands for Grip and Glide

Manufacturer	Brand Name	Dimension	Wax or Waxless	Core	Performance Observations	Other Observations
Karhu	Gazelle	54/49/52 mm Sidecut	Both		Good forebody flex	Versatile; in-track and off-track
Kneissel	Red Star	59/49/55 mm Sidecut	Both		Excellent turning ski	Used for off-track touring
Kneissel	Red Star Elite	47 mm Parallel Cut	Wax			In-track light touring ski
Lampinen	Lampinen MG	51 mm Parallel Cut	Waxless		A stable, general touring ski	
Rossignol	Frontier XL	60/50/55 mm	Wax		Stands up to vigorous use	For beginning skiers
Rossignol	Frontier AR	60/50/55 mm Sidecut	Waxless		Stands up to vigorous use	For beginning skiers
Skilom	142 LT Micro		Waxless, "Hairy Base"			Manufacturer claims that the base hairs are impervious to water saturation
Trak	Mariah	59/49/55 mm Sidecut	Waxless	Foam and Wood	Livelier than previous model	Used for in- and off-track skiing
Trak	Spirit W	59/49/55 mm Sidecut	Waxless	Polyurethane & carbonfiber	Easy to turn	Not a high performance ski, but adequate

Appendix Two
Racing Skis

BUYING SKIS is a matter of personal preference, but if you follow the chart from left to right you should be able to determine the best ski for your needs. Here are definitions of the terms used in the charts to facilitate your deliberations.

First touch. This is number of pounds of direct pressure required on the balance point to make a ski's wax pocket first touch the snow. You'll want a ski with a first-touch reading of at least one-half your body weight. Any lower reading will cause the wax pocket to drag on the snow when gliding on both skis.

Flex distribution. This measurement simulates glide on one ski under the full weight of a skier. The numbers in the table reflect pounds of pressure transferred by the skis to the snow; the higher the number, the softer the ski's midsection. Softer tips are desirable on racing skis because they allow the ski to track easier and absorb irregularities underfoot more efficiently. Tails should be stiffer than tips to track well, but too stiff a tail will dig into the track and drag. Heavier and stronger kicking skiers will prefer skis with fairly stiff midsections; lighter skiers and those still developing their kick and glide should opt for softer midsections.

Kick flex. This is the number of pounds of pressure each ski transfers to the snow under simulated kicking conditions one and one-half times the skier's weight). The higher this number in relation to the mid-flex number, the more kick is being trans-ferred to the snow. The ski should maintain its personality; if it's stiff in mid-flex, it should be proportionately stiff in kick flex. For instance, the Karhu Keviar U, stiffest in mid-flex at 11 pounds, is also the stiffest in kick flex at 52 pounds.

Torque. Torque values express a ski's resistance to twisting. Higher numbers indicate more torsional rigidity, and lower num-bers less torsional rigidity. Low resistance to torque is preferable for in-track skiing because it allows tips and tails to ease over track irregularities and follow sidewalls more efficiently. Consider the values in relation to each other: The tail should be more tor-sionally rigid than the tip, but not excessively so.

Weight. In the chart, the weight of a single ski is given (with-out binding) in grams.

Shape. Almost all racing skis are javelin shaped. Wider skis are slightly heavier, but more stable. Narrower skis are slightly lighter and, all other things being equal, faster, with less side-wall drag.

A Note on the Latest in Ultra-Light Skis

Fischer began the trend to light with their Air Composite Core RCS skis which weighed in at a paltry 1000 grams per pair.

Now Kneissel has developed a light ski—the 1000 VM Ultra Skis. These Ultras have a core of cellulose honeycomb covered with carbonfiber laminates on top and bottom.

Karhu has come up with an innovative approach. Knowing that most of the very serious racers have three or more pairs of skis for different snow conditions, this industry leader is mar-keting a package consisting of four different pairs of skis. Each pair is designed for different snow conditions, temperatures, and track conditions. The package offers:

Green Matrix Skis. These skis weigh a mere 1000 grams per pair and are designed with an elongated pocket and a hard, smooth base to work best in cold, powder snows.

Blue Matrix Skis. Blue Matrix skis are designed for older snow conditions. They have a black P-Tex Electra base which reduces icing at temperatures around the freezing point. The Blue Matrix skis weigh 1200 grams a pair.

Red Matrix Skis. Red Matrix skis also weigh 1200 grams a pair. They are for use on old, coarsely grained snow when it is cold or wet. They have a slightly stiffer camber and a micro-grooved base for added speed in sticky snow. The polyethylene sidewalls supposedly add durability.

Yellow Matrix Skis. Yellow Matrix skis have a multigrade wax-less base for warm days when you can't decide which wax to use.

There are also two other waxless newcomers on the racing scene: the Peltonen Zeta Ski and the Fischer Zero Grade. The Peltonen model has a machine abraded base. The Zero Grade by Fischer, also abraded at the factory, has a double thickness of base material. The double layer means that you can re-abrade the base in the kick area in order to create more "hairs" without worrying about wearing through the base.

Finally, Peltonen has developed a special ski for the "skaters" out there. It is called the Pro-S. Each ski has a rounded top profile so that it can be turned more quickly onto edge to begin skating.

RACING SKIS

Model	Flex distribution				Kick Flex	Torque		Weight	Shape			Base	Construction	Performance Summary
	First Touch	Tip	Mid	Tail		Tip	Tail		Tip	Mid	Tail			
Atomic Arc Wasa P	105	12.8	48	24.6	76	1.6	6.0	650	37	44	44	P-Tex 2000	Torsion-box construction with foam	Relatively high first-touch value and soft response. Excellent ski for the light or intermediate racer.
Edsbyn GTX 787	90	7.4	64	22.4	110	1.1	6.4	505	42	44	44	P-Tex 2000	Carbonfiber	Very light ski. Mid-flex value of 64 is ideal for average kickers as well as for serious racers.
Elan SR 020	120	12.9	22	22.2	64	1.6	3.0	630	37	43	43	P-Tex racing base	Foam and air-channelled poplar core	Narrowest ski. Ideal for skiers up to 240 pounds with a high first-touch value of 120. For new racers and aggressive recreational skiers.

Model	Flex distribution				Kick Flex	Torque		Weight	Shape			Base	Construction	Performance Summary
	First Touch	Tip	Mid	Tail		Tip	Tail		Tip	Mid	Tail			
Epoke Honeycomb Comp	95	12.4	52	26.0	106	2.8	7.2	622	41	44	45	Polyethylene	Aircraft aluminum honeycomb	Most torsionally rigid at both tip and tails. Good ski for beginning racers or advanced recreational skiers.
Fischer RCS	115	13.3	36	26.3	88	1.6	4.4	658	41	44	44	P-Tex 2000	Graphite reinforced air channel isocore	Proven on world cup circuit. Rated medium overall based on test values. Ideal for lightweight, experienced racers or aggressive recreational skiers.
Jarvinen Kevlar 56	85	10.8	60	23.2	104	1.8	4.8	597	39	42	41	P-Tex 2000	Fiberglass sandwich, air channel foam	Quite soft in first-touch and mid-flex values. Suitable for experienced and accomplished lightweight skiers.

| Model | Flex distribution | | | | Torque | | | Weight | Shape | | | Base | Construction | Performance Summary |
	First Touch	Tip	Mid	Tail	Kick Flex	Tip	Tail		Tip	Mid	Tail			
Karhu Kevlar U	150	13.1	11	22.8	52	1.5	3.4	650	41	44	43	P-Tex 2000	Carbonfiber laminate with Kevlar foam	Stiffest ski. High first-touch reading of 150 pounds. For heavy or strong kicking skiers.
Kneissel Superstar Vario	130 125	11.2	20 16	16.2 18.4	70 60	4	2.4	672	39	44	44	P-Tex 2000	70% fiberglass, 30% polyurethane	Adjustable skis provide variations in flex and first-touch characteristics. Suitable for powerful skiers.
Peltonen Kollen	95	9.7	48	22.0	88	1.2	3.6	573	34	44	44	P-Tex 2000	Polyurethane Core	Very lightweight. Average values from tip to tail. Good ski for semi-serious racers.
Rossignol Silver 44	100	13.4	44	22.2	104	1.8	6.4	665	40	44	44	P-Tex 2000	Acrylite foam core	Slightly softer-than-average mid-flex and kick flex values. Melamine sidewall construction increases glide.

Model	Flex distribution				Torque			Weight	Shape			Base	Construction	Performance Summary
	First Touch	Tip	Mid	Tail	Kick Flex	Tip	Tail		Tip	Mid	Tail			
Skilom Carbon 155	150	11.0	48	27.8	60	2.6	7.0	630	41	44	44	Polyethylene	Carbonfiber rabbelbox core	Has stiff kick flex values, high first-touch reading. Most torsionally rigid tail. For strong skiers and serious racers.
Trak Top Competition, Stiff Setting	165	12.4	15	18.0	60	1.2	3.4	670	38	44	44	Sintered polyethylene	Synthetic foam with strips of fiberglass	Adjustable skis. Very stiff in mid-flex values. High first-touch value and relatively heavy weight. For strong, experienced skiers.
Trak Top Competition, Soft Setting	150	12.4	4	20.6	68	1.2	3.4	670	38	44	44	Sintered polyethylene	Synthetic foam with strips of fiberglass	Adjustable skis. Very stiff in mid-flex values. High first-touch value and relatively heavy weight. For strong, experienced skiers.
Average	120	11.7	35	22.3	79	1.7	4.8	627	39	44	44			

Special Acknowledgment

In this, your 111th year, all cross-country skiers applaud you, Jackrabbit, for showing us a better way of life: your way. We are only now beginning to appreciate your personal crusade to preserve our land, the native way of life, and ourselves. We are fortunate that you stationed yourself in our midst, and we thank you. Very few of us will ever take a snow bath, sleep out in the snow without a tent, or be able to hunt, fish and cross-country ski with your expertise, Jackrabbit, but we appreciate your achievements. None of us will ever measure up to your high standards; however, we can assure you that we will endeavor to carry out your wishes to the best of our abilities for ourselves and future generations. Your spirit will always be with us.

Index

Beginning to ski: developing cardiovascular fitness, 44-47; developing skiing ability, 50; on-ski training, 49-50; pre-skiing exercises, 43-48.

Bindings: see Boots; Boot/binding systems.

Boots: and bindings, 20-22; telemarking, 74, touring versus racing, 20. See also Boot/binding systems.

Boot/binding systems: ALS system, 23; choosing, 25-27; versus conventional boots, 20-21; Contact system, 22, 27; Control system, 22-23; racing, 25-26; Salomon system (SNS), 21, 23-24, 26-27; touring, 25-26.

Canadian Ski Marathon, 92-93.

Children: beginning touring, 77-79; Jackrabbit Ski League, 95-96; learning to ski, 50; selecting skis for, 15-16; suitable clothing for, 32.

Citizen versus elite racers, 91.

Climbing techniques: herringbone, 67-69; parallel side step, 69. See also Racing, uphill techniques.

Clothing: for back-country skiing, 32; children's, 32; innovations in, 32-33; layering, 31-32; powder suits, 33; racing suits, 33-34, underwear, 31-33.

Competitive events: Alberta, 94-95; British Columbia, 95; elite versus citizens' classes, 91; Manitoba, 94; New Brunswick, 91-92; Newfoundland and Labrador, 91; Nova Scotia, 92; Ontario, 93; Quebec, 92-93; Saskatchewan, 94.

Diagonal stride, 56-57; compact, 119; variations, 57-58.

Downhill technique, 55; racing, 120-121.

Etiquette for skiers, 50-52.

Falling, 60.

Fitness levels, 44-46, 49, 106-111.

Flat-terrain techniques: see Diagonal stride; Racing, flat-terrain techniques; and Skating techniques.

Food and drink, 34, 76.

Gatineau 55 race, 98-104.

Herringbone, 67-69, 119-120.

Hypothermia, prevention, 31.

Kick and glide, 16, 56; racing, 114-116.

Marathons: author's experience of, 98-104; planning for, 87, 90; training for, 87-89.

Poles: baskets, 29-30; composition of, 29; grips and straps, 30; innovations in, 30-31; proper length, 31; selection of, 31; shafts, 29; tips, 30.

Poling techniques: with diagonal stride, 56-57; double poling, 57; racing, 115; racing double poling, 116-117.

Pre-race training: interval training, 112-113; marathons, 88-89; on-snow, 112-113; uphill techniques, 113. *See also* Training.

Racing: double poling and, 116-117; downhill techniques for, 120-121; flat-terrain techniques for, 114-118; herringbone techniques for, 119-120; kick and glide techniques for, 114-116; pacing, 123-124; Peaker Pump technique for, 117-118; planning for, 121-123; poling and, 115; skating techniques for, 120; turns, 117; uphill techniques for, 118-120; waxing for, 120-121, 122. *See also* Pre-race training.

Racing skis, *see* Skis, racing.

Roller skating, 48-49.

Roller skiing, 47-48, 109-110.

Seniors, and cross-country skiing, 82-84; learning, 83.

Skating technique: full skate method, 58; half skate or marathon skate, 59; and racing, 120.

Skier incentive programs: children's Jackrabbit Ski League, 95-96; "Count the Kilometers," 96-97; touring distance awards program, 96.

Skis: base, 18; camber, 16-18; children's 15-16; composition of, 17; construction of, 17-19; fit, 16; flex, 18; length, 17; racing, 19-20, 235-241; sidecut, parallel cut, or negative sidecut, 18; telemarking, 73-74; touring, 232-233; waxless, 15-16, 18-19.

Slowing down and stopping, *see* Snowplow.

Snowplow, 59-60; and turning, 61.

Smith-Johannsen, Herman "Jackrabbit," 9-12, 33, 243.

Spring skiing, 126-128.

Telemarking: equipment for, 73-74; learning, 71-73; and sidecut skis, 17-18.

Touring: advice for beginners, 75-76; family, 77-79; family vacations, 79-81; non-competitive, 75-81; waxing for, 75.

Trail etiquette, 50-52.

Training: cycling, 108-109; muscular fitness, 110-111; orienteering, 107; roller skating, 48-49; roller skiing, 47-48, 109-110; running, 46, 106-107; ski bounding, 107-108; ski striding, 108. *See also:* Pre-race training.

Turns: kick, 66-67; moving step, 65-66; parallel, 63, racing, 117; snowplow, 61; standing step, 63-65; "Stem Christie," 61-62. *See also:* Telemarking.

Waxes: basebinder, 37,40; hardness, 42; innovations in, 41-42; order of application, 40.

Waxing: basic, 36-38; and camber, 38; chart, 38; equipment for, 37; progressive techniques, 41-42; and racing, 120-121, 122; and skiing conditions, 37-38; and skiing technique, 38-39; and touring, 75; and type of ski, 39; typical application, 39-40.